the broken letter
divorce through the eyes of a child

a novel by carl lawrence
forward by raul ries

The Broken Letter
Divorce Through the Eyes of a Child
© 2000 by Carl Lawrence

Published by Shannon Publishers
PO Box 575
Artesia, California 90702

Shann Publ@AOL.com

photos by Dodgen Photography

SHANNON
PUBLISHERS

Printed in the United States of America

International Standard Book Number
0-9638575-2-5

Dedicated to Kenny W., Mike M., Mike D., Dave N., Nicholas P., and Robee N...

...who lived it
- I only had to record it -

FOREWARD
by RAUL RIES

I remember watching my youngest son, Ryan, rack the billiard balls for another game of eight ball, thinking to myself, he's become a man. Is this the same little guy I used to toss in the air and wrestle with on the living room floor? Where did the time go?

"You're up, Dad," Ryan said. Call your shot."

Call my shot? I thought. Okay. Your brothers and you are all kids again. And I get to start over as a dad, but knowing what I know now after all my years of mistakes.

My wife Sharon and I had taken Ryan with us for the day, for a special time as a family just to talk and relax. A friend had recently given me a copy of Carl Lawrence's, The Broken Letter. I sat down to do some relaxing reading. I was wrong.

I didn't get past the second letter from Randy to his AWOL dad when I felt a tightening grip on my throat and a grieving pain in my heart. All these years after the fact, I felt the same embarrassed loneliness that Randy describes as I remembered my own strained and painful childhood relationship with my father. I knew exactly how Randy felt, and I began to weep.

Page after page of unanswered letters stabbed

at my heart. I thought of all the kids today who have been abandoned and left to fend for themselves because of selfish, neglectful fathers who refused to grow up and live a committed life of responsibility to their families. The pain turned to anger as I thought of today's young people foolishly mimicking the drug-crazed hippie generation of the 60's, but this time around the idealistic search for peace and love has been replaced with senseless hatred and violence without apology.

Carl Lawrence hauntingly and starkly illustrates the breakdown of the American family and how today's "fatherless generation" has been given little hope for the future. It is my prayer that God use this powerful book to convict all fathers of the tremendous need to invest their time and effort into their childrens' lives. Without the men of this nation making a stand for righteousness, our country, along with its kids, face a bleak future.

This is a sobering book for every American family.

Raul Ries
Calvary Chapel Golden Springs
Diamond Bar, California

The effect was hauntingly surrealistic as the lights from cars, turning on their way home, invaded the quiet bedroom, casting dancing shadows across the walls.

The light revealed a slight figure sitting up in bed on a pillow against the wall, a yellow writing pad resting on his knees, and a ballpoint pen in his hand. He wasn't an athlete and never would be. He tried with everything he had to be one because that pleased his dad, and pleasing his dad made him happy. His sensitivity and personality showed themselves not only in the straight A's he had always earned in school, but also in his voracious appetite to read anything and everything - from the newspaper to the encyclopedia. In this, he was more like his mother, who had always wanted to go to college to study literature. Instead, she had married early and given birth to him following a "six month pregnancy."

His hand reached up and rubbed eyes that burned from a long evening of television. The eyes that used to sparkle with happiness and anticipation were now red and bleary, too weary and burdened for a twelve year old.

"Nuts!" The word came as though it had been rehearsed many times. He reached out and turned on a light by the side of the bed. It was a light made from a worn-out skateboard, the kind of thing a mechanically-minded father would make for his only son.

The light cut across the face of Randy Scott Maxwell. His short hair, bleached blond from the sun, stood out in several directions. His orthodontically perfect teeth bit into his lip. He held his burning eyes shut for a few moments, then tightly pressed his lips together. His eyes, which seldom reflected fear or anger, now were deep pools of loneliness.

With a long sigh he reached down and picked up the ballpoint pen which had dropped to the floor, then propped himself back against the wall. He sat for a moment, then hit his head in frustration against the wall. He uttered a few words that might have been profanities, but they weren't loud enough to be heard. He didn't want to wake his mother who was asleep in the room across the hall. She needed all the sleep she could get. Three months ago, her world, like Randy's, had fallen apart late one evening with the words, "I'm outta here," the slamming of a door, the sound of a car spinning its tires as it pulled out of the driveway, and then, silence.

The normally comforting and quiet sounds of a house at rest became loud and unbearable. Who would fix the refrigerator if it stopped its familiar hum? What if the furnace didn't kick on during the winter? Dad always handled those things - "Mom and I don't have any idea what to do," he thought. The waiting in Randy's world had changed. For so many years of his life Randy had heard the key turn in the door and would shout, "Dad's home!" eagerly running to meet his father. Or if his dad came home late, Randy would pretend he was sleeping and wait for the kiss on his forehead and the whispered, "Good night, Son."

As he lay alone at night, he searched his mind a million times. What had happened? How could something so good have become such a terrible mess so quickly?

He couldn't kid himself. He had been aware that the voices had gotten a little louder. There had been the angry slamming of doors. Then, one night, when Randy got up to go to the bathroom, his father was lying on the couch - fully dressed.

Then suddenly, with that final slamming of the door and squealing of tires, Randy had become a part of the fatherless generation.

He would tell himself it was all a bad dream, that he would wake up and everything would be all right again. Once again he would hear, "Time for you men to get up or you'll be late for the game." "Let's fix the car today and change the oil." "Let's move it!" But now, there was only silence.

The fear of waking up alone kept Randy from going to sleep.

He shifted the writing pad on his knees and began to write. Randy Maxwell, age twelve, who had to be cajoled, threatened and locked in his room to write, "How are you? I am fine. Thanks for the Christmas present," was now going to write a letter.

Slowly, he wrote...

April 20, 1991

Dear Dad,

I hope you don't mind my writing to you like this. I haven't written very many letters, as you know, so I may make a few mistakes. Also, I know you like people to mind their own business, but I'm not your mother or your wife, I'm your only son, so maybe I am your business, at least some of the time.

Don't blame Grams for giving me your address. She didn't. I was over at her house the other day, and I saw a big brown envelope on her kitchen table addressed to you. That was the first I knew you were in San Francisco, but I think Mom knows because Grams and she talk every day on the phone. Mom always talks about you in low whispers when I'm around. They do most of their talking in the evening when I am watching TV.

Anyway, I copied your address down when she went into the other room. Sneaky, huh? Sort of like the way you taught me to steal second base, when nobody was looking. Just kidding.

It's neat that you are in San

Francisco. Maybe I can come and visit you for a few days before you come back. We could go watch the Giants get blown away. Are you still a Mariners fan?

Well, Dad, it's been one month since you took off. I know, because I have it marked with little x's on the calendar you gave me to keep track of baseball and basketball practice and allowance day. Mom says you left on a business trip, but I still think that you left because you were mad at us. By the way, you're a lot more generous with your cash than Mom. With you gone nobody loses money on the couch when they take a nap. Sometimes it's slim pickin's around here, but we manage.

It's one-thirty in the morning, but I want to write this letter while I am thinking about you. For a week now I have been thinking over and over what I am going to write. In fact I've been doing a lot of thinking lately, but I won't bore you with it. I'm sitting up in bed with my pillow doubled up behind my head just like you used to do when you wanted to lie down and think things through.

That's what I do now. That's the way I go to sleep at night - when I can sleep - and the way I wake up in the morning - with a sore neck and a tired brain. At least I'm only a pain in the neck to myself and not to Mom and you. I think over and over and over again, what the heck happened to us? I have asked myself a thousand, jillion times whether it was my fault. Was it my fault dad? If it was, I promise I'll never do again what it was that made you want to get away from me.

I was thinking a couple of nights ago, what if I went to live with Grams for a while when you come back. That way Mom and you could spend some time together without me bothering you.

Then I get thinking about things I still want to do with you. The Mariners are doing great, but Griffey would hit better if we were watching the game together.

Fernando keeps asking where you are, but his dad hasn't said much. They have already filled your spot as third base coach, but only temporarily. I'm sure you can have it as soon as you get back. Let me know when you're coming for sure, and I'll let them know.

Mom is not very happy. She is quiet most of the time. I hate it when anyone phones her because she always ends up crying.

We still try to go to church, but everyone acts weird when we're around, like they can't think of anything to say. The people who always talked to us after the service sometimes even act like they don't see us, kind of like we used to do to the new people.

We walked up to the Grahms and the Larsons after last Sunday's service, and they all just said, "Hi," really fast and then took off for their cars. Nobody even asks us out to lunch at Denny's anymore. It sucks. I feel like a big geek there.

School isn't bad. Nobody knows yet that you're gone.

Sometimes I get this terrible feeling that you aren't coming back. That's when I pull the pillow over my head and try to forget. The nights are long and my brain won't turn off. I sure can't sleep very well these days.

I guess life isn't much fun anymore. I feel like I'm twelve years old going on 100.

Fernando's dad is really nice. He takes me with them on the way home from the ballgame to have a hamburger, but it tastes better with you. Besides, no one wants to share a giant 7-Up with me.

Some of the things I always wanted before, I don't want anymore. Remember how I used to want to get out of bed and join you for the closing sports on the 11 o'clock news, and then beg to stay up and watch part of Jay Leno? Well, now Mom goes to her room, and I sneak out and turn the TV on and listen to the sports, all of Jay Leno, and Conan O' Brien. But you know what? It's no fun. The only reason I do it is because it's better than going to bed and lying there, waiting for the front door to open, hoping you'll come home late from work. My ears hurt from listening at night for those sounds. I'm getting old, Dad. You'd better hurry up and get home or I'll be too old to talk to you anymore.

Love, your son,

Randy

P.S. I hope you notice that I sign my name with a broken R, just like you always did. You said your dad signed it that way, too. It's a tradition. Like father, like son, huh?

May 28, 1991

Dear Dad,

Hey Pops, you'd better hurry home, your old lady is losing it. Just kidding. But really Dad, Mom is acting weird. I got home from school today, and the front door was locked. I used the key and when I came in, I couldn't believe it. There, sitting at the kitchen table with your bathrobe on, was Mom. She had a half cup of cold coffee in her hand, exactly the way I left her this morning when I went to school.

I said, "Hi." She looked a little surprised and said, "Oh, are you home already?"

I told her, "Yeah, Mom, I have a ball game." She said she'd get me something to eat. I went to my room to get my uniform. I opened the closet door, and it wasn't hanging there like it used to be. I looked in the dirty clothes basket in the bathroom, and there it was, sweat and all, just like I left it when I threw it in there after the last game. I pulled it out. Man, did it stink. I tried wiping off some of the dirt and did the best I could to shake out the wrinkles and air it out. I put it on, but I was afraid to look at myself in the mirror. I remembered how you used to say, "You can stare at yourself all day, but you will only look like Ken Griffey, Jr. when you get out on the field and play your buns off, so let's go, slugger!"

I went into the kitchen and sitting on the counter was my hot dog. Actually, it was a cold dog on a cold bun, with no mustard, no mayonnaise, no chips, no Coke. I took it into the bedroom and scarfed it down. When I carried the plate back to the kitchen, Mom looked at me like I was from another planet. She looked at my uniform and was about to say something when I was saved by the beeping of Fernando's dad's horn. I ran out the door just as she was saying something. When I got in the car, Fernando said, "Wow man, did you play a game already?" His dad was more polite and reminded both of us that it wasn't the uniform, but the man in the uniform that counted. Sure.

I played a lousy game. All I could think of was Mom, you, me, and how things used to be. I almost missed my turn at bat, thinking how maybe I should go home and walk into the kitchen and massage Mom's neck like you used to do. Remember how she would smile and then feed her little pigs? But I'm afraid I'm the wrong Randy for that. She needs someone with big hands, or at least bigger than mine. Well, just thought I would keep you up to date so you will have a little idea of what to expect when you get home. Better hurry, Dad. Mom is getting flaky.

Love,

Randy

P.S. We lost the stupid game. Really I lost the stupid game for us. I forgot everything you taught me about sliding into home. Oh well, my uniform was already dirty anyway so it didn't matter. Eating a hamburger afterward (Fernando's dad pays for them), I told them I was thinking about retiring from baseball - getting too old. Who needs the pressure? Nobody laughed. They just ate a little faster. It didn't sound as funny as I thought it would.

P.P.S. Mariners are doing super - now, how about the Giants? I hope you're still a Mariners fan. I like being on the same team with you.

"Well, Mom won't have to worry about washing my uniform anymore. **I retired last night.**"

June 30, 1991

Dear Dad,

Well, Mom won't have to worry about washing my uniform anymore. I retired last night. I never was very good at it. It was no fun not having you, Mom, and Grams in the stands yelling. The hamburger and Cokes afterward, without you, tasted like the dirt I ate when I slid into base. You gotta admit Dad, there was no one on our team that could slide like me.

Anyway, I won't bore you with all the details, but last night I hit a good ball out to center field. I stole second - another great slide. Fernando hit a fly to left field and I ran for third, but everyone was yelling for Fernando, not for me. Another hit and I made it home. It tied the game. A few of the guys said, "Nice run, Randy," and "Atta boy," but the stands were silent.

Then someone else hit a two bagger, and Fernando took off from second. As he rounded third, his dad left the coach's box and stood at home plate yelling, "Come on Freddie! Come on Son, run!" Fernando collapsed into his dad's arms a few feet past home base. We won the game.

On the way home I realized there was no fun in bustin' my butt, if in the end there is no one at the game who really cares how I do anymore, and no Dad to congratulate his little hero. So I quit.

Your almost big league son,

Randy

August 11, 1991

Dear Dad,

Well, Jay Leno was boring, Conan O'Brien wasn't funny, and when Mom woke me up some dude was trying to sell me a juice mixer that was going to change my life. I crawled into bed and went to sleep, but like always, I woke up again, and here I am. I can hear Mom tossing and turning across the hall. Every time I close my eyes I think of terrible things. So I figure that I'll do something useful, like writing you a letter. My teacher says sometimes it makes you feel better to write things down.

Hope things are going good in San Francisco and that you enjoyed the 82 degrees you had today.

Before I try to go to sleep again I thought I would let you know the latest woes of the Maxwell household.

Actually, I'm writing because my English teacher said I was a good writer and that I should practice more. So here I am practicing, sort of like homework.

Actually, things aren't going all that well - or is that "good"? Anyway, let me tell you about a day with the Maxwells. Some new rules:

1. Don't answer the door. It will probably be a bill collector.
2. Don't answer the telephone. It will probably be a bill collector. They are everywhere.
3. Don't ask for spending money. There isn't any.
4. Don't ask Mom how her job interviews went today.
5. Don't ask Mom if you have clean clothes for school.
6. Don't ask what's for supper. But if you do, never, never, never say, "Oh no, not again!"
7. Don't say I'm starved. After all, you had a big supper two hours ago - or was that two days ago?
8. Don't say that Vanna White is pretty, or you hate Happy Days reruns, or that Oprah looks skinnier. And don't ask to watch baseball. Go out and play instead. But I've tried that, and it's not working very well.
9. Don't say I think I'll go over and see Grams just before it's time to eat supper.
10. Never, never, under any circumstances say, "I wish Dad was here then this wouldn't happen."
11. Never, never ask, "How did this get broken?"
12. Never, never, never, never speak without first thinking about what you are going to say . . . unless you don't want to live to be a

teenager.

Actually, Mom is great. I'm just kidding. But, now that I think about it, it has been awhile since I've had a good laugh. Oh, crap, Dad, let's admit it. Life sucks.

Last Sunday we went to church. I tried to pretend I was sick, but it didn't work three weeks in a row. Sunday morning fever, you know. The pastor talked about what heaven is going to be like, but he wasn't sure what hell would be. I can tell him. Hell is when you are sound asleep having a wonderful dream about a family living together, loving each other, watching TV, eating too much, hugging, kissing, answering the telephone with, "It's your dime, my time, so make it short," answering the door and finding the people that want our money are Girl Scouts selling cookies - which mom would always buy and tell us not to eat because they weren't as good as she made - but then waking up, and realizing it's all a dream. That's hell - it lasts Sunday through Sunday. It's life.

Remember the time we were coming home from somewhere, and we had to stop when a car hit a kid on a bicycle? The bike was smashed under the car, but the kid was standing on the sidewalk with only a few bruises. We got out and looked at the bike, then looked at him. People wanted him to sit down, but he said he felt fine. You said his ego was hurt more than his body. As we pulled away after the police came, you said, "Well, I bet it'll be a while before he rides a bike again." Well, Dad, my life is like that kid, and I'm standing on the sidewalk. People are asking me if I'm OK. I'm trying to say yes. I'm probably only bruised, but I hurt all over. I wish I was the bike.

Well, anyway, happy dreams - whatever they are. See you at the intersection.

Love,

Randy

P.S. Mom says I'm getting sourcastic - or however you spell that stupid word. Maybe I'm growing up and will be an adult like you before you know it.

Sept. 6, 1991

Dear Dad,

Just a warning. If you call and the operators say the number is no longer in service, don't be alarmed. They are right. It isn't. I wanted to go over to Fernando's house after school today so I called Mom. The operator said, "The number you are trying to reach is no longer in service." I tried again. Different operator, same message. I ran all the way home trying not to think of what might have happened. When I got there, Mom was sitting at her favorite spot at the kitchen table, holding a cup of coffee with both hands. She had just gotten home from another job interview. She told me the phone had been disconnected because we didn't pay the bill. At least SHE was still here. So now we have the telephone company, the gas company, the electric company, and the mortgage company as regular visitors. Kids selling girl scout cookies don't have a chance. We still have the garbage men coming, so I guess it could get worse, I think. Anyway, I wanted to warn you. If you call, better call Grams and she will let us know so that we can call you back from her house.

Sorry I don't know what the weather is like in San Francisco, or how the Giants are doing. The paper was one of the first things to go.

I wonder if you might do Mom a favor. I need some new socks for PE. Mine have holes at the heels and toes. Kind of embarrassing. I asked mom and she said she didn't have any money. I told her to charge them. She said she doesn't have a credit card. They were all in your name. How about sending mom one of your cards so she can buy me some socks. I'm sure there are a few things she could use too - like coffee, bread, milk - and some of the other things that we sort of got used to having.

Mom hasn't gotten a job yet. I heard her on the phone over at Gram's house last night - hers still works. Mom was saying, "Oh, sure, I can give them my recommendations. I can tell them I am very fast. I had a baby 6 months after I was married, but I have had three miscarriages since, so I have slowed down a little. I can't type, but I can write and I can add, boy - can I add. Come on over and look at the bills on the kitchen table. I have them all added up. But I don't perform miracles, and I've forgotten what it's like to write checks, so I can't do bookkeeping." And then she started crying and hung up.

She's really sad today. She's working hard trying to find a job and trying to keep me happy at the same time. I guess I'm not helping all that much. I guess when all is said and done I am pretty much of a brat. I can sort of understand why you bugged out and why someday Mom may want to do the same thing. I'm not the world's greatest prize for a son.

Well, Dad, sorry to bother you with all this kid's stuff. We still look OK from a distance, but up close, we stink.

Write.

Love,

Your stinker son,

Randy

Nov. 1, 1991

Dear Dad,

I'm sure this will come as no surprise to you - or will it? You are now the father of a teenager. I went to bed last night a kid and woke up a man - all 13 years of me. Didn't think I would make it, did you? I hope I'm like Grams. She says she's not getting older, but better, and you know, she is. She's so quiet and peaceful. When Mom cries, she cries with her. When Mom tells her she's OK and she'll make it, Grams encourages her. She tells mom how lucky she is to have a daughter-in-law like her, and they hug. But it's more than women's stuff. Her hair is getting gray, and she looks more tired than she used to, but she never loses her cool. We both have great moms.

But back to my birthday. I have to admit it was not the best birthday I ever had, and it was all my fault. Remember how on my birthdays Mom always surprised me in the morning, and you always surprised me at night so I could celebrate twice? Well, this time I didn't celebrate even once. But then at 13 I guess that kid's stuff gets kind of corny.

Mom woke me up and told me to hurry or I would be late. I looked at the clock. General Electric hasn't repossessed it yet. It was a little after seven and I usually don't leave the house until 7:45. I stayed in bed until Mom called me again. I got up, washed, and decided at 13 I wasn't quite ready yet to shave - but then you took the razor, didn't you? I killed as much time as I could, took my back pack and headed for the front door. Mom called, "Randy are you leaving..." I was out the door before I could hear what she wanted. When I got aways down the street I pretended my shoe lace came untied so I could bend over and look back. There was Mom standing at the door, holding my lunch. I looked at her for a second, stood up, and started running to school as hard as I could, not looking back.

I played a good boy at school. No one knew how rotten I felt inside. I kept asking myself why I felt so rotten. I didn't do anything wrong. I leave for school every once in awhile while Mom is still in the bathroom - no big deal. Why should I feel so rotten about today? When I got home the house was empty and quiet. Mom was out looking for a job. I went into the kitchen and saw why I felt so rotten.

There sitting on the kitchen table was an angel food cake, my favorite, with 13 candles burned down to the icing. Beside it was a folded napkin and a birthday card for "A Young Man." Sitting next to my chair was a half-empty coffee cup and a napkin all wrinkled, like it had been real wet. Now I really felt rotten. Thirteen and still a stupid kid. After all, this mess isn't her fault. It's probably mine.

I went to the fridge to take my lunch out and eat it, but I realized I wasn't hungry. I went to the mailbox. There were the usual overdue notices and threats of, "Give me your money or your life," but no birthday cards. Guess you are probably too busy. I understand.

Well, I tried to make it up to Mom, but I'm afraid I wasn't very successful. Then I went to bed, where I am now - though it's past midnight - writing this letter.

But I made one vow on my birthday. Now that I am a man, I will never cry again.

Happy birthday to me. May they get better when you come back.

Love, Your teenage son,

Randy

Nov. 10, 1991

Dear Dad,

You know that "greasy spoon" down
on Harvey Street where you would never let
us go? The one with all the pickups parked
around it, where all the customers look like
Willie Nelson? You called it the "low life
express." Well, you can go there now - no
more low life. It's upper class and the reason is they have a wonderful, gorgeous, new
waitress from 3 PM to Midnight, five nights
a week.

She's about five feet six inches, no
more than 125 pounds, and has light blond
hair. Her uniform is a little big - it belonged
to the girl that got fired the night before -
but she brings a new class to the place.
Every little bit helps.

You guessed it. Mom got a job. Not
the greatest, but she's working, and guess
what, we are eating. Don't knock it, Pops.
She has been there for a week now, so I
don't see much of her. I hear her when she
comes home at night, washes her one uniform, and then I can hear her count her tips
at the kitchen table. Sometimes she says,
"Is that all?" other times, "Not too bad." She

said the other day that she might also get a job in the kitchen down at the hospital during the weekends. She has all the bills out in the order that they are going to be paid. Most of them are overdue, but she's worked out some deals. It's gonna take a lot of tips. I hope those rednecks spend their money on something other than pickup trucks and gun racks. Well, anyway, when you come home, I'll take you out to eat - free.

Love, your over-fed little son,

Randy

Dec. 27, 1991

Dear Dad,

Well, we survived our first Christmas
without you. It wasn't a total disaster, but
man it sucked real bad. We could all have
won Academy Awards for the way we acted
happy and that nothing was wrong. I think
that you were the star of the show, even
though you weren't here. Grams was here
and uncle David, who got drunk again, like
usual. He brought his own bottle because
he knew that Mom wouldn't have anything
for him to drink. He was nice until he took
too many trips to the bathroom. Each time
he came out he was a bit more obnoxious.
He gave us a Christmas present, though.
He went into Gram's room, lay down on the
bed, and fell sound asleep - best present of
the night. Grams, Mom, and Aunt Debbie
kept apologizing for Uncle Dave, saying he
almost never drank, except on holidays.
Sort of like Gramps - every day was a holi-
day. I was a good boy and just sat quiet. I
remember how you used to do that now and
then when something really bugged you.
You bit your bottom lip.
Some of the people from church came

over and sang a few Christmas carols outside the door. I think the neighbors enjoyed
it more than we did.

Whenever someone would comment
on a decoration Mom would start telling
about it and then stop and leave the room.
Everything on the tree reminded Mom and
me of you. We either bought it for you or
you bought it for one of us or we bought it
together. I don't want to say that you were
hanging on the tree - only that you were
here, though you weren't, if you know what I
mean.

Christmas morning, when we used to
get up, pray, sing a few Christmas carols,
and open the gifts, was a real disaster.
Neither Mom or I sing too well. You always
had the best voice in the family. But when
we started, "Oh Come All Ye Faithful, Joyful
and Triumphant," I stopped and said, "Mom
this is stupid. I am not joyful. I feel ugly
and mean and wish it were the fourth of
July so I could go out and light a firecracker
and blow this whole stinking world up." We
opened the presents later that afternoon
before more people came for dinner. I don't
know why you adults feel that if you are
lonely you can just invite more people to the
house and that will take care of it.

I was sitting in the bathroom all by
myself when they called us to eat. The food
tasted like sawdust. Mom and Grams spent

hours preparing it - everything you like, but it was like we waited and you didn't show up so we went ahead and ate anyway, without you. We really didn't expect you, but it was Christmas and God gives special gifts. If He sent His Son on this day, why couldn't He have sent me a father? I guess I will never understand. But you know Dad, you don't have to understand to hurt. You can hurt without any understanding at all, and that is what I am doing.

After dinner everyone said they were full and went to lie down. We were all lying. We hardly touched your favorite, the fruit salad. Grams made it, Mom remade it, but none of us ate it.

Damnit, Dad, you ruined our Christmas. We just can't get over you. Every decoration on the tree and all the food on the table reminded us of you. And every time the phone rang, everyone looked at each other for a second, thinking, maybe it's Randy - the other Randy.

Well, anyway, its over.

Joy to the World - oh, sure.

Happy New Year,

Jan. 25, 1992

Dear Dad,

Mom got a second job. She works at the hospital, and it's not all bad. She works Sunday morning, so I don't have to go to church anymore.

Mom and Grams say I really need church, but I see enough people. I promised them I would go from time to time.

They were shaken up when I told them I was tired of hearing about a loving Father who lives zillions of miles away, who would come whenever I called. I can't get you to come and you are only a thousand or so miles away.

I told them I didn't believe in Easter bunnies, Santa Claus, or loving fathers anymore.

Mom cried, Grams looked hurt, and I stormed out of the kitchen, went to my room, slammed the door, put on my earphones, and turned up the music.

Now a true member of the fatherless generation,

Randy

"I was afraid to go to sleep because **I thought Mom would leave me, too.**"

March 2, 1992

Dear Dad,

You're not going to believe this. When I got home from school today, there was a big ugly sign right in the middle of our front lawn. Some dork stuck it there. You know what it said?- FORECLOSURE SALE. I couldn't believe it, our house for sale! I pulled the sign out and threw it into the bushes. We can't sell this house. This is our house. It's us. It's where all the memories are. This is where I spit food all over the kitchen, where I opened my first birthday present, where we watched the Super Bowl and Seinfield and ER. This is where we sat around and cried when Gramps died. This is where we plugged in our first stereo and heard the room filled with music. This is where we laughed, cried, and got mad at each other. This is where Mom and you fought for a half-hour and then spent half the night making up. We can't let them sell this house Dad, can we?

Dad, I promise you. Whatever it takes to not sell this house, I'll do it. I'll quit school and go to work at the Taco Shack. Tell me what I did wrong. Am I so bad that you want to destroy all the memories? Were they just stupid games to you? Well, they weren't to me. I spend hours every night reliving them. It's the only fun I have anymore. I promise I'll be the best kid ever born if you come home and tell them not to sell this house. I'll clean up the bathroom every time I take a shower. I'll swear on a Bible if you want me to. I'll go to Sunday School, to church, anywhere you want me to go. I'll work so hard at baseball practice I'll be a Ken Griffey, Jr. in 30 days or your money back. I'll mow the lawn without being told and wash the car every Saturday.

Dad, can't we sit down and talk? Come on home and we will take that For Sale sign, break it up, and barbecue some hamburgers. Please Dad, I've been a lousy son, but not anymore, just don't let them sell the house. I know Mom feels the same way.

Please,

Your son,

Randy

March 18, 1992

Dear Dad,

Well, it's been three weeks since I wrote to you last. Nothing much has happened around here. They have the FOR SALE - FORECLOSURE sign out of the bushes and stuck back in the middle of the lawn.

Last night was kind of a bad night, so I thought I would write to you today and get it off my chest. Sometimes that helps me. I have a tough time sleeping at night, but I finally went to bed, and began to sleep, I think, because I had a horrible dream. I heard the door close in the middle of the night. I thought it was you coming home, so I jumped up and called Mom to tell her you were home.

I ran to the door but there was no one there. I went in to tell Mom it was a mistake but her bed was all neatly made, and she was gone. I ran to the window and saw the lights of a car slowly pulling away like Mom does. She was leaving. I ran from room to room. I tried calling Grams, but the line had been disconnected. When I woke up, Mom was holding me, crying, "Randy,

Randy, it's OK. You're having a dream. Wake up." I was sweating like I was playing baseball in 100 degree heat. Mom was there!

I didn't tell her the dream, but after she went back to bed I began to think. I thought Mom might be thinking about leaving. After all, I thought as I lay my head on my folded pillow, Mom would really be a lot better off without me. She would not have so many expenses, like my clothes and food. If I were out of the way, it would be easier.

I guess the government could take care of me. After all, you have been paying taxes all these years.

I lay in bed shaking for a long time, my heart thumping like it was going to explode. I was afraid to go to sleep because I thought Mom would leave me, too.

Well, it's almost daylight. Mom didn't leave. I could hear her toss in her bed. I'm supposed to have a test in English, but I don't think I'll do too well. That's another thing Mom is on my case about. My grades have really dropped. I tell her it's because you aren't here to help with my homework.

Well, I'm sure you have your own problems without hearing from a crybaby in Seattle.

Let me know how things are in San Francisco. Maybe someday if Mom leaves, I can come live with you. Just kidding.

Love, your son, still at home,

Randy

May 1, 1992

Dear Dad,

Hope this letter won't be too long for you. If it is you can read half now and half later because I probably won't be settled in enough to write again for a long time.

I am lying on the floor of my room in my sleeping bag. Everything is gone. Tomorrow morning we move to Gram's house. Strangers bought our house, and strangers will be moving into this room - my room, our room. We didn't see the new owners. It was at some auction or something.

Mom made me pack all my own stuff so I could decide what to keep and what to throw away. I was sitting with baseball caps, gloves, some trophies - things you and I had collected all these thirteen years. I was swinging your golf clubs, which I am keeping for you, and wouldn't you know it, Mom walked in to tell me to hurry. The men from the church would be here in a little while with a truck to help us move. I sort of lost my cool and screamed at her, "I don't want to move! This is my house. This is our house!"

I sat down on the bed and yelled, "I'm

not moving. You can move, but I am going to stay right here." She walked over to me, put her hand on my shoulder, crying like she always does, and said, "I'm sorry. It hurts me too, but we just don't have the money. We just couldn't make the payments." I started using some words that I had never used before. I wasn't even sure I knew some of them. I told her to get the hell out of MY room and leave me alone. She looked more frightened than sad. As she walked out I heard her say, "Oh, Randy, Randy . . ." But I'm sure I was not the Randy she was talking to. When she yells at me to clean the sink out after I use the bathroom, or to take out the garbage, or to change my socks 'cause my feet stink, there is not doubt which Randy she means. But other times I'm not quite sure which Randy she means.

I packed. Actually, I threw everything into boxes. I couldn't stand to handle some of it, so I just threw it. The last thing I had to take off the walls was my Ken Griffey, Jr. poster. You were right. It did stick to the wall, but I took it off as good as I could.

So the men have come, taken all my stuff, and I am here for one last night. Mom is sleeping on the floor too, so I won't be alone. I'm not angry; I'm not sad. I guess I'm just numb, laying here looking at a piece of the Ken Griffey, Jr. poster sticking to the wall. Sort of like my life. Part of me will always be in this house and nothing can change that. That's the way it'll be when I put the poster up in our new house - it won't all be there. A part of me will always be in this room. This is where we wrestled every Saturday morning, where we built the trophy stand, where Mom would come and tell her men to come and eat, where we would move the TV and invite some of the kids in. Remember how Mom would fix hamburgers and we would watch the World Series?

This is the room where Mom and you came to sit when I was sick. You took turns so that whenever I woke up one of you would be beside me. Even though I was sick, I was never afraid. Right now I would rather be sick. This is where I had strep throat, or whatever that was, and you were deciding if you should take me to the hospital. I went to sleep and woke up better and you didn't have to. This is where it all happened. And now I have to leave it behind - with a little of me. I guess, like Ken Griffey, Jr., I'll never be complete again.

Randy

June 4, 1992

Dear Dad,

You won't guess where I am. I mean where I'm living, where I am lying right now, in bed writing this letter. Let me give you some guesses. There used to be a picture of Roger Maris on the wall. But that's gone now and part of Ken Griffey, Jr. is in its place. There is the same table and desk where some young blond dude used to sit with his mother standing over him so he would do his homework. There are a few stains on the carpet from glue where someone was putting together a model airplane and spilled the whole mess on the floor. That's right, Dad, I'm in your room. The room where you were raised in Gram's house. Of course, you weren't as lucky as me. I don't have a Dad who keeps coming home drunk at night like Gramps did, yelling and cursing.

Mom has her own room. Grams has hers. Grams still works at the store, so she is gone most of the day. She spends most of her spare time at church or sitting in her room watching TV. We've got a phone now and I can answer it. There's a TV and some of your old records. I listen to them. They sound pretty good. Things may be looking up.

Randy

July 6, 1992

Dear Dad,

Summer vacation is sure boring without baseball and you. On top of that, Mom is really on my case. I can't tell if she is mad at me, at herself, at the world, or just frustrated. She told me tonight that my personality is changing, and she doesn't like what I am becoming. Grams just stood there, but by the way she looked at me, I could see she agreed with Mom.

I am having this feeling - not so much of anger, but just a burning inside of me, sort of like bad indigestion. I feel like a car battery full of acid. I think a lot about whose fault it is that this family broke up. Maybe I am not the guy who is responsible, after all, but just the one who has to pay for it. I am the victim. I mean, after all, what did I do that other kids don't do, and their dads don't run off on them? When you guys fought, I always managed to get out of the way - to go to the store, to my room, or to see Fernando. I tried not to take sides, though sometimes you were really wrong and stupid in the things you said and did. So, Daddy-o, why blame me?

But that doesn't get rid of my indigestion or the burning in my gut. It's not like on TV - take a Rolaid and in 30 seconds feel like a new man. It's going to take a lot more than that.

Of course things could be worse. I have a friend named Dennis who is just a year older than me, and you won't believe what his folks did to him. They were both making big bucks as engineers in airplane factories. They lived in a big house, but they separated, and as soon as they started living alone they found new people to share their beds with. Neither of the lovers wanted this little twerp of a kid around. I guess he cramped their style. So, his dad and mother bought a condominium, right near the school. I wanted to go there, but he wouldn't take me. Now Dennis lives all alone in this nice condo. His mother visits a couple times a week to clean for him, do his laundry and bring groceries for him to eat, with plenty of TV dinners for the microwave. A little bit like our house, now that I think of it. Maybe that's part of the indigestion.

Anyway, he was laughing about how he is afraid to tell his mom what he likes anymore, because when he gets home, whatever he mentioned will be all over the place. He said that two weeks ago, he told her he really liked those new barbecue chips. When he got home, the place was filled with chips. He said he could have started his own store selling barbeque potato chips. But his grin disappears when he talks about the nights.

His mom is living with a guy who has a son just about his age. When Dennis goes to bed at night, all alone in his nice new condo, with his bags of potato chips, he gets so angry. He imagines his mom tucking in someone else's kid, and leaving him alone so that he can't sleep. He gets up and beats the bed. Then he starts knocking things off shelves. He came in one day and his mom was picking things up and asked if he was having wild parties. She didn't seem to care about the parties, only that they shouldn't get too rough. How wild a party can a kid his age have? Spill Coke on his pajamas or trip over the cord and pull out the plug of the VCR? That's pretty wild!

When I think about him, I think about myself. Maybe I would be better off if I threw a few things around. But it would only make things worse for Mom. She has enough problems. She works two jobs now. She leaves early in the morning and comes home late at night. If I got up late and went to bed early I would never see her. When she gets home, she comes in to see how I am, smelling of stale grease from the restaurant. She says she wants to buy a new home - that we shouldn't have to live with

Grams forever. By the way, even Grams seems to be changing. She doesn't understand me anymore, either.

Well, like you folks out in California say, "Life is a beach and then you die," or something like that. I just wish I could get off the beach part.

Randy

Sept. 28, 1992

Dear Dad,

    I started a new school. I like some of the kids. Nobody knows where I came from or anything, so with a few little lies, I tell them my dad is on a business trip to San Francisco. I lucked out. I have another super cool English teacher, Mrs. Myers, who goes to the same church that Mom and Grams go to. She welcomed me and said she was glad to have me in her class. She always puts a little note on my homework - like, "You are a good writer," "You are eloquent" (whatever that means), and she encourages me to write more. So that's why I am writing this letter - to practice.

    Well, life is different. Things are getting better, but I still miss my own house. Since your room is in the basement, it doesn't do me any good to lie awake and wait for the door to open at night - in case you come home. I would never hear it way down here.

Living it up in your old room,

Randy

Oct. 10, 1992

Dear Dad,

Well, we've kind of settled in with Grams. She seems to enjoy it more than Mom and me. She said she's not as lonely as she was when Gramps died. I left most of my stuff in boxes, so if we ever move to San Francisco I won't have to pack so much stuff.

I still my new school better than the old one where the kids I grew up with kept asking stupid questions like, "When's your dad coming home?" or saying things like, "My dad said your dad deserted you." I told this one kid if his dad had the brain of a rat he would know better. That was always good for a fight. They were all ugly. Glad those kids are out of my life. Here, I've found a group of kids just like me. We all go home to an empty house, our moms work, our dads have split, and we understand each other. None of us will ever be scholars, but we will survive, that's for sure, and right now that's the name of the game. I'm beginning to realize that is just like being an adult. Adults really don't give a damn as long as they get what they want. Well, I hope you are getting everything you want.

I don't see Mom too often.

Most of my teachers here are dorks, except, of course, Mrs. Myers who says she knows you. She is really nice. She told me yesterday I should write more - put my feelings down on paper - and she would give me credit for it. I didn't tell her that that is what I was doing. She's a real stickler on using the right tense, punctuation, and so on - things I don't pay much attention to, but she said if you want to pass the class you have to do it right. If she wasn't so nice I'd tell her to get lost, like I did my algebra teacher. He's about 25 and a real nerd. I think this is his first year of teaching. He acts like he's spaced half the time.

Well, when you get time, write.

Love, your scholar son,

Randy

November 1, 1992

Dear Dad,

Well, I am fourteen years old today, into my second year as a teenager. And what do you think Mom gave me, along with my favorite angel food cake and decorations? Would you believe a thesaurus? I've got to look at the cover of the dumb thing to spell it. I thought a thesaurus was a dinosaur that died millions of years ago - but not this one. Not just a thesaurus, but a Roget's Thesaurus - whoever he was - thanks a lot, buddy.

Here is mother nature pushing me into puberty, and dear old Mother Maxwell pushing me into college. At any rate, I am no longer lonely. Now I am "aloof," "rusticated," a "troglodyte" like some dude named - get this-Diogenes. I am also "estranged," "derelict," "deserted," and "untenanted." Just thought you would want to know in case you ever had to define your son. I take it I also have been "tactless," "impudent," and suffering from "blackguardism." All of that and I'm only fourteen years old. Can you imagine what I will be like when I get to the last page of this prehistoric gift?

It's time to go watch Jay Leno. So, this is your "querulous," "captious," "fractious," "peevish," son saying, not good night, but, "Au revoir." Let me sign it with a "nom de plume," though I would feel better using a "nom de guerre." I hope you are impressed - excuse me - "unctioned," "passionaized," "pulsated," "palpitated," and most of all, "rapturous."

Oh well, maybe next year she'll buy me a dictionary.

That will be a gift that I can really use - or, excuse my ignorance - a gift to which I can "devote," "dedicate," and "consecrate" myself, which will be not just "instrumental," but "subservient," "utilitarian," and "pragmatic."

As you can probably tell, I don't think Mom will ever understand me.

Love,

Randy

Feb. 6, 1993

Dear Dad,

I know you're really going to be mad at me, but I couldn't help it. Mom took some of your things and put them in a jewelry box on top of her dresser. She took a bottle of Musk and an old razor, just waiting for you to come use them again. I guess she hasn't given up, either.

Well, I took your ring - the one you got in Vietnam, or Nam, as you called it, the one with the name of your ship on it and the blue stone. You would never tell me much about where you got it, only that it is all you want to remember about Nam. I held it and it felt like you were right there for a moment. I could almost hear you tell me not to touch it. I felt you close, so I carried it downstairs to our room. I didn't want to set it down, so I did what I know will make you mad. I carried it around on my thumb until I got to school. Somehow it made me feel a little closer to you. I was hoping that by taking it, you would be home when I got there. Then I would give it to you and you would do what you said you'd do if I ever got into your box - whoop my little butt. This new kid who is real friendly, David, saw it and asked what it was. I said, "Nothing but a ring," and stuck it in my pocket. He wanted to see it, but I told him to mind his own damn business. I swear once in awhile when Mom's not around. Makes me feel a little like a man. Hey, I'll try out the Thesaurus. I could have told David to mind his own "confounded" or "cursed" business. No, I like "damn" better.

In English class, I took the ring out several times and looked at it. I guess Mrs. Myers saw me because when the bell rang, she asked me to stay for a moment. When the room cleared, she asked me to come to her desk. I just stood there as she looked at me and said, "It's your dad's ring isn't it?"

"What ring?" I asked.

"The one in your pocket. The one you kept taking out to look at."

I admitted it was and told her you brought it from Vietnam. She asked if she could see it. She handled it like it was something very precious. She said, "Hold on to it. Carry it if you want. Don't ever be ashamed of it." As I turned around to face her, she put her hand lightly on my shoulder and with tears in her eyes, said, "My husband and I had a son in Vietnam, but he never came back. Oh, a part of him did, but they never let us see him. He was in a box with a flag on it. Only 19. Davis is with the

Lord; we know that, but it still hurts. We don't even have a ring. Now, from time to time we go out to Memorial Gardens and place some flowers on his grave. We talk about him and what kind of girl he would have married, what he would look like now. He was our only child. You lost a dad; we lost a son." Then she took my hand, and with more tears in her eyes, said, "It's 'OK,' Randy, to grieve when you lose someone you love. It's OK to cry. It's OK to remember all the good things. Carry that ring with you; think about what a good man your dad is. Don't ever forget him." She looked right into my eyes and said, "You lost a dad; we lost a son, but it's OK to cry." I didn't cry, but Dad, I have the ring right now, right here - your ring.

Thanks Dad, for being my dad. We had some "bonzer," "swell," "crackajack" good times together.

Your son with the little fingers,

Randy

Every morning I tell myself that **today is gonna be different.**

April 10, 1993

Dear Dad,

Every morning I tell myself that today is gonna be different. It's gonna be cool. I'll wake up feeling stoked. I'll jump out of bed in a hurry to get somewhere and have some fun - and for a few seconds I think its gonna happen, and then the loneliness and anger just kind of take over. Even if I was going to jump up, grab something to eat and meet the guys at the mall, I wouldn't have the energy. I just feel tired. I can't sleep, but I'm never sure I'm awake either.

I was lying here thinking about it last night, and I remembered Waylon and Willie. Remember the day we brought them home - those two little pups looked so much alike. We named them after your favorite country singers.

Mom wasn't very happy. She could handle one dog, but not two, and insisted that we get rid of one as soon as they were old enough.

Willie and Waylon did everything together. They rolled on the floor; they attacked me when I got down on my knees. They ate together and when one finished, the other would follow him away. They slept together and got up together. They chased cars as they got older. They even wet on the floor together - and that was when Mom said, "Enough is enough. You have to get rid of those dogs."

Then someone at your work had a son who lost a dog and he was so lonely that you wanted to give him one of ours. I cried, saying they loved each other - they were like twins. Sometimes it was hard telling one from the other. But Mom's prodding and you being a nice guy outweighed my crying, and we gave Waylon away.

I remember when you picked him up and took him to the door and Willie started barking. When Waylon was gone Willie just sat there and stared at the door. After that, every time it opened he would run to it and wait. When it opened and it was only a human, he would slowly make his way back to some other room. He looked at me like, "You gave him away. You gave Waylon away. I don't want to be around you anymore." I couldn't get him to wrestle anymore. We almost had to force him to eat. We took him to the vet, and he said he was grieving over Waylon. It was too late to do anything about it. By now, the kid was so attached to Waylon, we couldn't take him back.

I don't think Willie ever forgave us. He just lay around and seemed to lose interest in living. I bet if he had been in school he would have stopped doing his homework. He would not have cared anymore about where dogs came from, how they arrived on our shores, or how to count dog biscuits or anything like that.

Then, one day, the doorbell rang and Willie didn't come running. It was the neighbor telling us that Willie was in the middle of the street when old, blind, Mrs. Johnson came around the corner from the grocery store. Willie never even tried to get out of her way. He said it was like Willie almost wanted to be run over. He didn't want to live anymore. I remember going out and picking him up. He just looked at me like, "Now are you happy?" Then a day later he died. But I think he died the day we gave Waylon away. Life lost all its meaning ("sense," "purpose," "significance," "definement," "explication") for him.

Well, I gotta go. Think I'll go out and walk in the street. Maybe old, blind, Mrs. Johnson will be driving to the store. Maybe ....

Randy

July 16, 1993

Dear Dad,

It's amazing how things change. A couple years ago I could hardly wait for summer and would dread even thinking about going back to school. Now it's just the opposite. It's the middle of July, and I am counting the days 'till school starts. Weird, huh?

When the only baseball you now have is a few hours on TV on a Saturday afternoon, and the only possibility of a vacation is if it rains too hard and I can't get home from the mall for a couple of hours - things get pretty desperate.

I've tried to read a few books, but they don't seem to be very interesting. Couldn't even get into your Louis L'Amours. But even if I did like them, I wouldn't dare discuss them with my friends. They'd chase me out of the arcade at the mall - the only place I go. Trouble is, I'm always broke, so I just have to stand around and watch other kids shoot aliens out of the sky.

Most of the time when I'm awake, I just lie in my room staring at the ceiling. I feel lonely and pissed off. I could really care less about life at this point, what good could possibly come out of it anyway?

I used to be able to daydream about what I wanted to be when I grew up. Now I'm not sure I even want to grow up.

Why should I daydream about girls, having a family, a home, and a good job when I'm not sure there will ever be a tomorrow?

I saw your old bow and arrow hanging in Grams' garage the other day. You were going to teach me how to use it. I took it down, only to find the string was broken - that's me, broken.

It sucks when a nobody really wants to be a somebody but doesn't know how. I would give anything to hear a few of those words that used to make me so mad, like - "Son, you can't spend all summer sleeping. Let's go change the oil in the car."

So I wait, and wait, and wait - until the first day of school and something to do - some place to go.

Your waiting son,

Randy

Sept. 8, 1993

Dear Dad,

Well, I blew it again. I went through some stuff above the garage and guess what I found? Your high school yearbook and even better, your Navy sea bag. I brought it down to my room and went through it. I found your Navy blues. Man, did they look cool, so I put them on. They were a little big, but not much. Even the white hat was there.

I looked at myself in the mirror. I looked exactly like the pictures of you when you were just a little older than me. I could have passed for you if I had a few whiskers on my face.

Grams and Mom were sitting in the living room watching TV when I made my entrance. I walked in and snapped to attention and said, "Randy Maxwell, Jr. Seaman, U.S. Navy, reporting for duty, Sirs . . . I mean, Mams."

Grams looked like someone had taken all her blood out. She said, "Randy, my God . . ." Mom looked like someone had kicked her in the stomach. She jumped up for a second to run towards me, to hold me, and then stopped half way. "Randy? Randy..." I realized right away I was the wrong one. Grams got mad. "Why did you do that? Where did you get that?" Mom didn't ask - she just yelled, "How dare you do this! What are you doing with your dad's things? You get out of here right now and change those clothes." Grams looked at me like - I understand how you feel, but that was a stupid thing to do.

I guess this is one more time when I see I'm still a stupid kid who turned a good evening into a disaster. But that is about par for the course. You're lucky you're missing this period of my life.

I went to my room and took off your uniform and folded it. I rolled the pants like I found them and put them back in the bag. There was also a short blue Navy jacket. It fit even better than the uniform. Your name was stenciled on the inside. It looked like it would be nice and warm. I took it and a black stocking cap and put everything else away in the sea bag and slid it under my bed.

I went to bed, feeling like my old self again - junior terrorist, always blowing up the family with my little grenades. I don't plan it that way. It just happens. After I was in bed, Mom came in and tried to apologize, but I pretended that I was sound asleep. I had heard enough.

Your sailor (almost) son,

Randy

Oct. 10, 1993

Dear Dad,

I have this problem - a man to man problem. I can't talk to Mom - she wouldn't understand - Grams, she wouldn't have to wear make-up for the rest of her life. She'd turn permanent pink.

Getting right to the point. I'm not makin' out, but I sure do have the urge, "inspiration," "prompting," "insistence," no - urge is still the best word. You know what I mean.

I used to wait for the swim suit edition of Sports Illustrated because we use to kid man to man about it. Now, when it comes out, I won't be able to look at it at the liquor store where I thumb through the other magazines we used to get at home - unless I want to get arrested.

I think totally horny might describe your quiet, "subdued," "solemn," "tacit," "passive" son who used to think the only thing you got from girls was cooties.

I didn't want to talk to our school counselor, an old woman - at least 30. One look at her and the urge would lose its surge.

So, I made an appointment to see the coach. He seemed to like me back when I had him for PE. He wanted to know if I was going to be repeating his class again, but I told him I had a bigger problem or "dilemma".

I stuttered for awhile and then began to explain that my body seemed to be just one overactive gland. He listened for a few minutes, and just as I started giving details, he said, trying to be serious and not show his impatience, "Randy, you're like every kid on my team. You're no different - only they get rid of some of their frustration on the playing field." He stood up, reached into his top drawer, and pulled out three little round packages that looked like half-dollars wrapped in foil like the Hershey kisses you used to buy all the time.

He said, "Welcome to the joys of manhood - use these." And then he said he had a ball team to coach and left the room.

I knew what they were. We have posters up in school that say with AIDS around, we're supposed to use them.

I guess, Dad, what the coach said was, do what your body tells you to do. Have all the sex you want, just be careful. There were some words on each package. Use for the prevention of disease. Is sex a disease? Is using a rubber a treatment? Are babies a disease? If I wear these things, does that mean that no one will get hurt, and I can just jump on and off like the monkeys we used to see in the zoo?

I walked home the long way so I could drop those things in the gutter, one at a time. Better that they be in the gutter than on me.

Help,

Randy

November 17, 1993

Dear Dad,

Now about that problem with lust. I just finished taking the longest shower of my life. I must have used up a whole bar of soap. Some parts of my body seem raw. Mom was knocking on the door to see if I was all right. I couldn't tell her the truth, so I'll tell you.

This girl Sheila and I sat beside each other in one of our classes. She seemed real nice. We talked about things we had in common. Her folks are divorced. One day in social psychology class, the teacher was describing the nuclear family that we each belong to. Afterwards, we talked about it and realized that what happened to both of our "nuclear families" is they hit nuclear mass and that we are part of the fallout. We both laughed, but we could tell neither of us thought it was very funny. We kind of needed each other.

Mom keeps talking about some of her friends as "kindred spirits." I never quite knew what that meant before, but now I do. It's someone who not only understands you, but someone who will stick with you no matter what happens. That's the way Sheila is. She dropped by the house once and Mom met her and liked her. I went to her mother's house and met her mom who was nice, but her step dad was a real dork.

When I went to pick her up for a date, her stepfather warned me, in no uncertain terms, that we were only 15, and not to forget it. I think he was afraid we'd act like adults. I wanted to say, "Hey man, if you are an example of an adult, you can be sure we won't act like you.

It was our third or fourth date. We went to a friend's house for a little party. The parents were gone. It was a really nice house. You could have taken ours and put it inside this one. The bathroom was bigger than our living room. There were bedrooms all over the place, and they all had beds - not just love seats that make into beds - but honest-to-goodness beds. We all sat around and smoked.

We broke off in pairs. Dad, I didn't mean for anything to happen, but in an hour it was all over. Sheila wouldn't speak to me on the way home. I asked her if she was going to tell her stepfather. I could tell by the way she looked at me we shared a secret. I went home and headed for the shower. Somehow my body looked different. It looked dirty. It wasn't; I had a shower before I left, but it felt dirty. I turned the

water on as hot as I could stand it and started scrubbing down. Halfway through, with
the hot water running on my neck and still
lathering myself down, I suddenly thought,
what if Sheila is pregnant? I wanted to run,
but there was nowhere to go. How would I
tell Mom that I was going to be a father?
What would Sheila's stepfather do to me?
After about 30 minutes in the shower, I
dried off. I still felt dirty.

So here I sit. What a dork I am - a
real loser. I have heard the guys bragging
on Monday mornings in the PE shower, but
I'm convinced that those that brag about it,
don't do it - they only want to make you
think they did.

Dad, I really need someone to talk to.
Oh man, if Sheila is going to have a kid, I
hope there is room for one more person in
California.

2 hours later - 2:50 a.m.

I have lost something that I can never
get back. I am not or never will be the kind
of person that I think I really want to be. I
have lost another piece of myself. This time
I tore the poster off the wall myself, and left
a little piece sticking there. The picture is
getting smaller and smaller. I don't want
anyone putting their arms around me, saying, "That's OK, everyone does it." I don't
need someone telling me it's OK. It's not. I
need someone to tell me why I did it and to

make sure that I don't do it again until the time is right. I can't go into Mom's room and say, "Hey Mom, guess what I did tonight?"

I'm not tired, but I am worn out, so I guess I'll try to get some sleep. Thanks for listening, Dad.

I lost a good friend tonight - the first one I've had in a long time.

Not ready for prime time,

Randy

February 3, 1994

Dear Dad,

Well, I have learned two things this week that are going to take a lot of hassle out of my life. I learned how to get through school and how to get along at home without all the hassle from teachers, Mom, and Grams.

First, school. I have this algebra teacher, who has us spend all our time trying to figure out what X means. Our relationship was like an undeclared war, but he finally called me up after class and said, "Look, boy, I'll make a deal with you. You don't screw up anymore in class, and I'll pass you. Take a test like everyone else, and somehow I'll find something right about your algebra. Maybe not the final answer, but somewhere in the test, and I'll pass you with a D. You can get your algebra out of the way, and we'll be out of each other's hair. You'll always be as dumb as hell, but you can work at a fast food place where you can use a machine that adds for you. So, we got a deal?"

What's true with algebra is true of the whole school. I am stupid; others have been telling me this. Just don't make any waves, they say. Just have an understanding with the teacher. Don't give them any trouble, and you won't have to study or do homework. Just come in, sit down and be quiet, and you'll pass. Then go to the mall and have a blast. So I'm going to pass this semester after all. Not with A, B, or C's, but what the hell? So what if a D is a little closer to the bottom than it is to the top? However, none of the above applies to Mrs. Myers. She's cool and she makes me want to work.

Now, about getting along with Mom and Grams. I took the stereo into my room. I borrowed a pair of earphones and now I can turn the sound up as high as I want. Pearl Jam, Nirvana and I get along really well. They understand me. They are my peers. No more hassling. Something bugs me, can't sleep - I just turn up the volume. When I get lonely I listen to the words and sing along.

Your rockin' son,

Randy

April 5, 1994

Dear Dad,

Today I lost another good friend. I never really met him, but I understood him and he understood me. When he sang, his loneliness and rage could have been mine.

Mom and Grandma hated when he sang in our house, but I felt like he was able to scream out what I couldn't put into words. I'd put on your old ear phones and play him as loud as I could. It kind of felt like therapy or something. When the tape was over and I'd sung along with every word I knew I wasn't alone. Someone else was as scared and angry as I was.

I heard his father went on a long trip too, and he's still looking for someone to help him understand what the hell is going on in this world.

Today Kurt Cobain killed himself. Dad, he had everything! Millions of people loved him, and no one was going to kick him out of his house. If he can't sort it out, how will I?

I know Nirvana is only a rock group, but they were my rock group, and now they're gone, too.

Randy

April 23, 1994

Dear Mrs. Maxwell,

I regret to inform you that we in the Counseling Department feel that your son has an emotional problem. We see in him tendencies toward lying, when telling the truth would be just as easy, and toward manipulating, when he is faced with reality. We see, also, that he has a general tolerance for deviance, impulsivity, and a need for instant gratification.

Your son's teachers report that he runs the gamut from depression to almost uncontrolled enthusiasm, usually depending on whether he has just entered the classroom or has been there for a period of time. It is our opinion that he is probably using some addictive drug, perhaps methamphetamines or cocaine, for energy and to help him during times when he feels either high or low.

People like this student generally seem to lose touch with the world around them. Your son spends much time in class daydreaming. He says that nothing bad is ever going to happen to him.

The danger is that with the use of methamphetamines, which unfortunately is readily available around campus, larger and larger doses are required as the nerves which it activates become desensitized to the drug.

This student needs help. We have no specific

drug abuse program here at the school, though our athletic coach has been counseling some of the students who participate in sports. Our recommendation is that you seek out a professional counselor or drug program for your son as soon as possible.

James Farrady

Director of Counseling

April 25, 1994

Dear Dad,

I got home from school early today. I
cut a class in history again, since I didn't do
the homework anyhow, and there was a letter from school to Mom. It was marked
important and personal on the outside, so I
opened it.

I'll attach it so you can do what you
want to do with it. Mom will never know.

I'm not Randy, just "this student." It's
a form letter, Dad. That's how much they
really care.

Am I out of control? Sure, my grades
have dropped a few points. Well, maybe
more than a few. But I am in control. I can
still do the things that I have always done.
I just don't want to do them anymore. I'm
beginning to grow and my legs ache from
growing pains. I need more sleep. When I
come home from school, what's wrong with
lying down and taking a nice long nap?

If I was on the honor role, Mom would
get a personal letter congratulating her, and
they would even use my name. Now, they
think that I am a doper and they send a
form letter. I have a feeling that they send

out a lot more of these letters than they do
the others. If I go to the coach for counseling, what will he do? Reach in his pocket
and hand me some cheap speed at half-
price? How about my algebra teacher? My
class is at eleven o'clock, and he is almost
always zonked himself by then.

This is part of society today, Dad, just
like demonstrations and banners were part
of yours. The only difference is, we don't
have to go to Woodstock to get our kicks. We
can do it in any of the bathrooms at school,
or in my room with my stereo. So what's so
terrible about that?

I can't ask Grams. She wouldn't know
what I was talking about. She still drinks
soda water for indigestion and puts ice
cubes on the back of her head when she gets
a headache.

So I've found a friend that can help.
It costs me $10.00 a pop, and he's there
when I need him. He tells me rock and roll,
sex and drugs, are what life is all about. So
here I go.

Help, one more time,

Your out-of-control son,

Randy

"It was just
another of
**life's great
rip-offs.**"

November 8, 1994

Dear Dad,

Mom has been really sick lately. She hasn't been to either job for two weeks. We don't have any medical insurance so she has been going down to the County Hospital.

Last night, just before Jay Leno, Grams said Mom was bleeding a lot and we had to go to the hospital right away.

I went into her room. She was white as a ghost. I could see she needed help. I told her we were going to the hospital, and she didn't say a word. She knew she had to go. Grams got her long robe - the one you bought her for Christmas four years ago - and while Grams helped her out of bed I went out and backed Grams' old car out of the garage.

Grams practically carried Mom to the car. I helped her in and then gave Grams the keys. She handed them back and said, "I'll sit in back with your mom. You drive."

Remember how I used to beg to steer the car just around the block, or when I would sit behind the wheel when you were washing the car and pretend I was driving. Now it was for real. I don't even have a permit. Got to have a "C" average for that - but Mom had to get to the hospital.

It wasn't as hard as I thought. I didn't stall the engine once. When we pulled into the hospital Grams told me to take her to Emergency. I guess I have driven by the hospital hundreds of times and the Emergency sign always looked comforting - kind of assuring that help was always there. That was because I'd never been inside.

Grams helped Mom while I went to find a parking space. I actually drove around more than I had to because I hoped when I walked into the hospital Mom would already be taken care of, and I could just relax. Wrong!

When I walked in the door some wimpy security guard stopped me and asked where I was going. I told him and finally - after looking me over and deciding I wasn't going to steal all the syringes and drugs - he let me in.

There were about twenty people sitting around on plastic chairs, some holding crying kids, some pressing down on bloody bandages, a couple were sleeping. I saw Mom. She was over in the corner. Grams had her arm around her holding her up.

When Grams saw me she said, "We don't have insurance so we have to wait for the emergency doctor."

I pleaded with the receptionist behind

her little glass partition, "Please get help. My mom is really sick. Look, I'll get some money somewhere - she could bleed to death."

She looked me right in the face and said, "Hey boy, everybody in this place is sick or they wouldn't be here, so relax and wait your turn."

I yelled, "She's bleeding to death!" But she turned to take information from a woman with a kid in her arms who - would you believe - had a tummy ache and wouldn't quit crying.

Grams told me to stay with Mom while she went to call some people from the church to pray.

I sat down beside Mom and held her head. She grimaced when I said, "Church, hell, why doesn't she go up to that window and tell that old prune face you need help?"

An hour later anarchy reigned. People kept coming with bleeding heads or crying kids, but none were as sick as Mom. Some even finally left. Do you know how long three-and-a-half hours are when you are standing watching someone you love bleed?

Each time I was sure they were going to take her next, an ambulance would pull up and all the doctors - both of them - followed the stretcher down the hall, leaving us sitting there.

I know what I did wrong. I should have run that damn car into a telephone pole and then they would have taken care of her.

Finally, they called Mom's name. Both Grams and I had to help her up. As we began to walk away, I heard a kid go, "U-gh-h-h." I turned and saw a pool of blood in Mom's chair. I wanted to pick up the chair and throw it in the face of the woman behind the glass.

A nurse told us the rooms were full so Mom would need to wait on a stretcher in the hallway. They would get to her as soon as they could.

Another hour passed. All Mom said was, "Oh, I'm so sick, I'm so sick. It hurts so bad - worse than the miscarriages."

Pastor Barnes arrived, took one look at Mom, and started pushing the stretcher toward the door. "Let's get her out of here." As we got near the door, old prune face said, "Where are you taking that patient?"

Pastor Barnes picked Mom up with both arms and almost shouted at the nurse, "To a hospital before she dies." The security guard moved to block him, but Pastor Barnes' "holy" glare caused him to step aside.

Thirty minutes later Mom was in a room at St. Jude.

Pastor Barnes said the church will

take care of all her expenses. He said we should have called him in the first place.

Finally, at 5:00 in the morning, he drove me back to County Hospital where I picked up Grams' car. As I looked at the Emergency sign, I knew I would never again find it comforting. It was just another of life's great rip-offs.

I'll keep you posted. Mom still loves carnations and See's candy. Better yet, you know how to get to St. Jude - remember, your only son was born there.

Love, your only son,

Randy

Dear Dad,

Well, you didn't make it in time.
Maybe San Francisco Airport was fogged in.
Anyway, it's all over now.

The school counselor came and got me
out of history class. When she walked in the
door, I knew who she wanted. When I
walked out of the room there were a couple
of hoots from some guys. One guy yelled, "I
told you not to stash that stuff in your lock-
er!" I could hear the laughs as I followed
the counselor out the door. I knew it would
probably be the last laugh I would hear in a
long time.

As I walked into the office, Pastor
Barnes stood up, put his arm on my shoulder and quietly said, "Your mom wants to
see you."

Neither of us spoke on the way to the
hospital. I can't tell you what went through
my mind. I don't remember traffic or anything. I just remember walking into the
hospital room. They had taken all the tubes
and machines away. Mom looked like an old
woman. For a second I thought it was
Grams, but she was standing on the other

side of the bed holding Mom's hand. Mom slowly turned her head toward me. Tearfully, she tried to speak as she reached to find my hand. I leaned over, squeezed her outstretched hand, and touched her forehead.

Her lips were dry and cracked. She slowly opened them, and I could barely hear her say, "Randy, my son, I'm sorry. Forgive me." I leaned closer to her face and told her she was the best mom in the world and there was nothing to forgive.

She tried to smile, as I kissed her on the cheek. Funny - as I did it, horrible guilt came over me as I realized how long it had been since I'd done that.

I heard her say, "Goodbye, my son..." Then she turned her head and looking straight up, sighed, "Oh Randy, Randy." I knew her last words weren't for me. Then, Dad, she just closed her eyes and was gone.

Grams held one hand, and I held the other. Pastor Barnes put his arm around me. I looked down at Mom. Oh, Dad, she looked so old, so tired.

I said, "Goodbye, Mom," and Grams began to cry. I thought to myself, she'll never again bake me another birthday cake. Never again will she come in my room and pick up my dirty clothes to wash and iron. Never again will I feel her warm lips kiss me in the middle of the night while I pretend I'm asleep. Never again will I see the light in her room go off just as I slam the door when getting home at three in the morning, and never again will I hear her quietly sob in the middle of the night. I realized I would have given anything to hear her say something that bugged me, like "Randy, what happened to the sparkle in your eyes? It's gone."

After one final look, we walked out into the hall. I asked Pastor Barnes if I could be alone for a few minutes. Grams and he stood aside as I slowly walked down to the elevator and pressed the button marked "Maternity."

A few minutes later, I stood staring through the glass partitions of the nursery that you looked through sixteen years ago - to see the nurses taking care of your new and only son, Randy Scott Maxwell, Jr. And now, Mom is not the new mother a couple of doors down, resting after giving me life. She's laying on a slab, dead, worn out, waiting for someone to carry her away. And you're in San Francisco, doing whatever it is you do with your life. There I stood. A new father came up to the window and a nurse brought over a brand new baby and held it up for him to see. He started talking to the baby. I can't explain the anger that consumed me. I wanted to grab him and say, "Don't just stand there. Go in and get that kid and take him home. Don't let anything come between you. Take him, hold him, never let him go." But I didn't. He looked about like you probably looked when you stood in that same place. I just looked him in the eye and said, "You don't deserve it, you old bastard."

Just as he was about to respond, Pastor Barnes arrived, put his arm around me, turned me around, and guided me to the elevator. He drove me back to the house, which is no longer a home.

As I lay here, in your old room, I realize the only difference between where Mom is laying right now and where I am, is that her slab at the hospital doesn't have all these stupid trophies, and a torn poster of Ken Griffey, Jr.

I wish that I would just die, too. Would you forget me?

Randy

Dear Dad,

These last couple of days have been a blur. I've tried not to think. I've almost worn out a couple of CDs.

Grams' house was a zoo. I was even afraid to go to the bathroom for fear I would run into a stranger.

Every place I turned there was food. I could have pigged out for a year. I guess I ate some of it, but I don't remember.

Then on Tuesday afternoon Grams and I were alone for a little while and one of those big limos came by and picked us up and took us to the church. We sat in the front row. I tried not to think of the good times we had as a family when we sat just a few rows back. You really seemed to like it then. What happened? Oh well, never mind. There was some music, but the best part was when people got up and told how Mom's life had affected them. A little girl in her Sunday school class got up and just said, "Mrs. Maxwell loved me even though I was ugly." An old man stood up and told how his wife and he used to hate to eat at the restaurant where Mom worked, but they had no car and it was the only place close. But when Mom came to work she made them feel loved and important. Then he took out a piece of paper and said, "This is her work schedule. We always planned our meals around it, and on her day off, we ate at home." Then he began to cry and sat down.

As I sat there I realized that there was a part of Mom I never really knew - or maybe I knew, but in my self-pity I had blocked out. Is that what you did?

Pastor Barnes gave a little message. I didn't pay too much attention to the Loving Father stuff. Then someone sang a song about no more pain, no more sorrow. I knew damn well they weren't singing about me.

When it was over they left Grams and I alone with Mom for a few minutes. Oh Dad, she looked beautiful. Grams dressed her in a white dress, and there was almost a smile on her face. She didn't look anything like she did at the hospital. She looked like her old self.

We took her to the cemetery. But I don't remember too much about it.

Pastor Barnes took us home. More food and more strangers.

I went into Mom's room and closed the door. As I sat on her bed, I looked at the two pictures on her dresser - one of you in uniform and one of her taken on her wedding day.

I carried Mom's picture into my room and closed the door and held it for awhile.

When I put the picture on my nightstand, there was, what I always called "her book," my thesaurus. I slowly rifled through it to see if I could find words to describe Mom. There weren't any.

Picking up the photo again, it suddenly dawned on me that she looked just like she did at the church - a beautiful bride waiting to be taken into the arms of her bridegroom.

Oh Dad, we lost a beautiful lady.

Randy

March 9, 1995

Dear Dad,

Your son is about to become famous - well, at least for twenty minutes, five more than most. Once every year the PTA asks one of the students to address them at their big annual banquet. Mrs. Myers is the speech teacher, so they asked her to pick a representative student who - get this - "holds great potential for the future."

She chose me. I was stoked. I told her I'd have to talk it over with Grams. She was more excited than Mrs. Myers. I still said no, but she asked me to do it as a memorial for Mom. "Sort of a closure on your mourning," she said. Couldn't resist that.

So, come Friday night, my first step to literary fame. Mom won't hear it, so I'll send you a copy. Wish me luck.

Your son, who "holds great potential for the future"

Randy

March 10, 1995

Dear Dad,

This is going to be kind of short. I want to finish and get out of here before Grams gets home from hearing the famous address of her grandson. Man, Dad, I blew it big time. I rehearsed that sucker. I let Mrs. Myers read it. I did research, even wore my necktie that I hadn't worn since Mom's funeral. Maybe there is a message there, I don't know. But, for sure, I won't be back at the PTA for awhile - like a couple of thousand years.

I got up, shaking all over - Mrs. Myers said that would pass - and began hitting with my statistics. I told them how many of their teenagers would kill themselves this year; how many would gain weight, but would lose it all at one time in the maternity ward or in an abortion clinic; how many of their dear little sons and daughters would be going to class stoned. They looked like, "Yes, we know; we read the paper, too." So then I told them to stop looking at us - I really meant me - and telling us teenagers, "You've got this wild hormone problem, so will you just stay out of trouble, eat the food

I put in front of you, and let's get back
together in a year or two when you are more
normal?" None of them laughed.

I thought I could get them on my side
by telling them to "burn our buns" once in
awhile, that we want someone to tell us
what to do. No response. Like, "Can't we
get on with the real business of this meet-
ing."

I could feel the anger welling up
inside. I looked at smug Mrs. Wendell and I
wanted to shout, "Hey, woman, let me tell
you something, your sweet daughter Cindy,
well, if she doesn't stop makin" it with every
guy in the parking lot, she's never gonna get
a diploma, but a grave marker - ever heard
of AIDS?" I saw Gary's mother sitting there
rather smugly. I wanted to step down,
shake her shoulders 'til her jewelry fell off,
and yell, "Your son lives in the bathroom -
where do you think he's getting all those
fine clothes? How come you gave him his
own phone number? Did you notice he has a
beeper he hides under his pants?" And
there sat our dear algebra teacher, and I
wanted to point to him and say, "Hey folks,
you want to get your kids into college? Then
they want a good mark in algebra and
geometry. I'll tell you how to do it. Make
sure that your kids see Gary in the bathroom before class and buy old teach at least
one good bag of weed, and he'll make sure of

a "C" average."

But I didn't do any of that. I just felt
all the years of anger and loneliness well up
inside of me. I was about to cry, but I didn't
want to do that. I looked at them and said,
"Please, folks," or something like this, "look
at me. Don't do to your kids what my dad
did to me." Still no response. Then I did
something that probably woke all of them
up. Remember when we were one run short
of being in the city tournament? We had
two outs, a man on first and the last man up
to bat. Good old Jose threw one right down
the middle, and crack, home run - no cham-
pionship for us - season's over. And you
turned to us on the bench and all you said
was, "Aw crap," or something like that, and
walked to the car. Well, I said it, but there
was no car. There would be no screeching
tires as I took off on my own, but I did run
out the door. I knew I had to find a rest
room. I ran into the bathroom and lost my
supper in the stall. As I was there I heard
the fast click, click of Mrs. Myers as she
walked down the hallway. With my dessert
whooshing down the toilet, I went to the
sink and washed my face in cold water. I
heard the click, click of Mrs. Myers walking
by again, only this time she was walking
real slow. I could hear her sigh something
and use my name a couple of times.

Anyway, I screwed up big time. So,

this may be my last letter for I don't know how long. I'm leaving a note for Grams that I have made life miserable enough for her, and I'm out of here - got my sleeping bag - ready to head for downtown. Like father, like son.

Your first class screw up son,

Randy

"**Loneliness disappeared** in a haze of sweet smelling smoke."

July 10, 1996

Dear Dad,

This letter is going to be a bit long, so bear with me. It's been a long fourteen months since I bothered you with the latest episode of America's number one misfit.

I tried life in the fast lane - or "sex, drugs, and rock and roll," as you guys call it in California. I just picked up my sleeping bag one night, joined up with my friend Dennis, and headed downtown. After that I lived under freeways, in the back of cars, in flop houses (though they don't like kids), an old abandoned house, and sometimes in parks. We showered at Greyhound depots 'til they kicked us out, the athletic departments of colleges - that lasted for seven months - but of course we only showered once a week - make that every couple of weeks. When the weather was warm we slept outside. When it was too cold (45 degrees is the official "shelter weather") we would check into the National Guard Armory for the night, but back to the streets in the daytime.

How did we eat? Two ways. We stole and we sold. We stole what others had, and sold what we had and others wanted. I won't go into any lurid details. You'll just have to take my word for it. It wasn't much fun. In fact, it was no fun at all.

It's a lifestyle I don't recommend. But society says, "It was your choice. You didn't have to live like that. Yeah right!

Let me explain how it happened, how the circumstances sort of dictated the lifestyle. I know you're not big on A.A., but let me take one of their lines: "Hello, my name is Randy, and I am addicted to more chemicals than most drug stores carry. Film at eleven."

Let me tell you about it, Dad. I know it's been 14 months, but I am still your son. The former I'm sure of, the latter may be open to some question. I'll strip my little epistle of all the drug vernacular and tell it to you in terms that you can understand.

The first time I tried drugs, I was fifteen - which is ancient for that kind of an adventure. Mom, Grams, and I were getting along pretty well, and a part of me really knew that they were treating me okay, but I still felt lonely and angry. I hadn't had a good night's sleep since the night you almost tore the door off the hinges and the asphalt off the driveway.

Little by little I began to run with some guys who had the same problem. They weren't quite sure they wanted to accept me, so I had to show them I was one of them. We went over to one guy's house one day after school. When we got there he pulled a couple of cigarettes out of his sock. They were small and twisted at each end. He said a guy in the senior class had given them to him - usually he had to buy them.

He lit the cigarette and passed it around. We all took a few puffs. I wasn't so naive to think it was a Camel - though it smelled a lot like one. I didn't know how to inhale, but I pretended. When they started to laugh, I imitated them. They would start telling something that happened in school that day, and then halfway through, they would forget what they were saying and we'd all laugh and hit each other.

They wanted to go to sleep. I told them I was so tired I could hardly move and I'd better go home while I could still walk - so I left. I never inhaled, I didn't know how, but just the acceptance of these guys was so great, I walked home feeling high, and I was in a good mood all evening.

Two weeks later, we cut our final class and went back to this kid's house. He said he had spent four bucks on some real good stuff - "Didn't we want to share it with him?" Even if I didn't, I couldn't let on I was scared so we laid a couple of towels under the door so the smell wouldn't go out into the hallway, in case his mom came home early. It was OK if his dad came home, because he always has a couple of "smokes" while watching the news, and he'd smell up the whole house anyway.

This time I inhaled. I laughed. I forgot what I was saying halfway through a story. I inhaled my first pot, but, oh man, it was not going to be my last.

First, we'd do it once a week, then twice a week, then almost every night. I was loving that deep warmth of the sweet smoke, followed by the burning in my lungs. When I would exhale, after holding it as long as I could, all the stress, the tension, fear, worries, hassles of life left me. Loneliness disappeared in a haze of sweet smelling smoke.

The euphoria of that first time it happened was unbelievable. I could laugh without stopping, and then half way through, get tired. Then I could go home and sleep a dreamless sleep like I hadn't done since we came home late from a Mariners game, and you undressed me and put me to bed. I could sleep 13 to 15 hours. Mom and Grams began to notice, but by now I was becoming a pretty good liar. I told them I was feeling contented at last and had begun to accept my life as it was.

I began to need more pot - but now I had to start paying for it. I not only became a good liar, I also became a good thief. Your

Nam ring kept all three of us laughing for a week.

At first I could cope - act normal - but little by little people began to see something was wrong. They knew it, I denied it, and there was that unspoken understanding that existed probably between a quarter of the kids in our school and the teachers and parents. All except one. Mrs. Myers knew. I could see it in her face. She never came right out and said so, but she would say things like, "You keep falling asleep in class. Are you getting enough sleep?" She would especially notice that my eyes were more red than blue and sadly comment on their sparkle being gone, along with the infectious grin I was once known for.

Then one day the counselor called me in and asked me out right. By now I was an accomplished liar, or at least a practiced one. She gave me a warning. Cool it. Don't stop it, just cool it. Pot users are hard to recognize unless they are under the influence at the time, so I managed.

Then Mrs. Myers asked me to give that famous speech to the PTA. If I had had the confidence in myself that she had, I'd be President by now. I've written about what happened after my great oratory exercise at the PTA. That's when I took my sleeping bag and split. I wrote Grams a short note that I had hurt enough people, and I was going to say goodbye to Mom one more time, then I'd get out of her life. Grams deserved some time away from me.

We lived during those first few weeks to smoke pot. No one hassled us. We were now a family so a lot of the guys and girls shared with us. I belonged. We were one - or so we thought. We didn't seem to have any of the terrible problems of addiction that we had heard about. There was no vomiting after a great high. I didn't wake up with one of those day-after headaches like I had when I stole a quart of booze and drank it all in one night. Most of all, there was the togetherness. And we had it as long as we had the pot.

But after a couple of weeks, even during the highs, we weren't really together. We would go out and search for food together, but when we got back to our pad we sat and ate it alone. Those who had Walkmans sat by themselves, listened to their music, and were alone with their thoughts. When the last roach clip was empty, we became even more separated. My old heavy feeling of isolation came back - though I was in a little room sharing everything I had, with people I thought were my best friends - I was really alone. I began to realize that what I wanted wasn't really marijuana, it was love. Not sex - we had that - but love.

One day Dennis and I were walking

down the street, and we ran into an old friend from school we called "Good Old Tom." He always had money, but he wasn't good, he was a dealer - in the heavy stuff. He tripped out with us a few times on our "kid's stuff," and always let us know he had something better. He asked us when we were gonna grow up and really fly. We told him we were ready but didn't have the money. He made us a deal. He needed a headlight for his car. He knew where there was a car just like his which had a light like he needed. He also had a couple screw drivers in his car he would let us use. He said he'd give us a "quarter" - twenty five bucks in our language.

A couple of hours later we gave him the headlight, but instead of giving us the money so we could buy kiddie stuff, he gave us some "crank," some "speed," some "rush," - methamphetamines to you. He even showed us how to use it. We got back to our pad - a vacant apartment which we would get into by crawling through a basement window. We were the only furniture.

As the three of us sat in a circle, Tom pulled out a small mirror and set it on the floor. He reached in another pocket and took out a couple of straws that were cut in half. Then like a king unwrapping a pearl, he reached into a pocket inside his jacket and pulled out a little plastic bag full of white power. "You want to live, Dudes, start living."

We knew what to do, and we did it; put the straw in our noses, held the mirror between us, and began a brand new life. There was no great rush like the first time. This was more genuine. It seemed to touch every part of my body. To hell with friends, food, sex, forget it - I found me. Of course, I didn't know at the time it was part psychological, part baking soda, and 1/10th methamphetamine. I knew when two "lines" were gone I had found what I needed. The problem was I was partly right. I almost had a rerun of the euphoria I felt the first time I smoked. We found out we could take speed and still function. But it was expensive, so we had to get jobs. We weren't that good at stealing.

We hung out in the park, and as we talked after a snorting session, we decided we had arrived. We were going to get jobs, buy some new clothes. The only person I saw around was the big dude with the tattoos who cleaned up the park. He never spoke, but only smiled at us. He never hassled us; he was always just there. I went up and asked him if he knew where I could get a job. He smiled and said the fast food places were the best place to look.

A week later I was working in a grease bucket. Wasn't very glamorous, sweeping the parking lot, washing off tables after a bunch of pigs finished eating, but it did one thing. At the end of each day the manager would place $20 in my hand - cash. I'd thank him, tell him I'd see him tomorrow. He'd say, "Sure kid, I'll believe it when I see it."

I would take off looking for plain old, nice, respectable Tom. I always found him or one of his friends, bought what I needed and went home. Sometimes Dennis, who had a similar job, would already be there with the mirror and the straw. By then, we had expanded our horizons to include coke and just about anything else that would take us away. If I was late, he'd already be tripping. In a few minutes, as my hands shook in anticipation, I would be inhaling what had now begun to feel like fire. Then I'd get so tired I couldn't move. I didn't bother to eat. My plane flight ended, my heart stopped racing. I no longer felt like I was going to explode. The gentle massage I got from the top of my head to the bottom of my toes began to subside. I'd go to sleep.

I'd wake up several hours later. It would be dark. I would wonder where I was. First thing I did was light a candle and see if I had snorted the whole line. If so, I would snort the straw to see if there was a grain or two left. And then, since the money for the drugs was gone and I couldn't get more until the next day, there was that awful feeling of loneliness. I blew the candle out. Maybe the darkness would help. Then I started shaking all over, and I'd light the candle again. I needed some light. If Dennis was there I didn't notice. We never talked, unless it was how to get more drugs.

We never did anything that didn't have one ultimate end: getting high. Of course, we could stop anytime we wanted. We felt like life owed us these little pleasures. On our day off we would go to the park - for one purpose only - to find someone who wanted to share some drugs, any kind. We didn't care.

But we weren't addicted - just living out a stage of our life. When the big tattooed dude came by he asked us how we were doing. We'd tell him our jobs were going fine. He just smiled and kept on walking. He knew better and so did we, but that was part of the scene. We had lied and stolen to get where we were, and we couldn't admit we had lost all control of our lives to half a straw and a bag of baking soda and white powder.

People walking in the park, except the tattooed dude, probably thought we were two boys whose greatest crime was being too lazy to work. In reality, we were totally controlled by our drugs and the deceit behind them. We were living a life of hopelessness and deception, and nobody seemed to care.

After a couple of months of this, my loneliness got worse so my drugs got stronger and cost more. They no longer produced euphoria; they were simply a way to get through the day. I not only thought of getting high all day long, I also dreamed about it at night.

Then one day something happened. I told a friend of old Tom's that I couldn't afford his stuff anymore because it was taking so much to get me really high. He introduced me to a friend who he called a real scum bag. But I was assured this would end my quest for that first-time euphoria, and that it would take care of me forever. He was almost right.

I know this is getting long and probably boring, but Dad, try to see it from my point of view. I was on a journey through a deep dark tunnel looking for light. I thought I had found it in marijuana, but the light went out. Then the darkness only intensified my loneliness, and I was angrier than ever. I blamed everyone but me.

I hoped, would you believe, I really prayed that LSD would be the answer. I made my first acid purchase. You could get it in different forms, but this was just half a pill. The dealer called it a "microdot" - something like you would buy in a drug store. I swallowed it.

It was only moments and something began to happen. The euphoria was almost there. This was going to be it. Now I had really found my new god.

I was looking for light at the end of my tunnel, and I saw beautiful bright lights. My perceptions of everything multiplied. I was floating, free at last. I looked at my candle and wondered, "Why does that glow? What is it that makes light?" It was like someone removed all the barriers to the secrets of the world. I saw people dancing up the walls. Slowly the world went into remission, and so did I.

The next day at work I felt different. Before, I had wanted to know what life was all about, but I didn't understand it because it was all outside of me. Now, it was inside of me. I was filled with light, or so I thought.

What I didn't realize was that was not the way others saw me. I was fired from my job for being unbearable, insolent, and some other things I won't repeat. But it was OK. They didn't understand me. Some day I'd come back and buy the old grease bucket, tear it down, and build a skyscraper.

But little by little, the beautiful images and the light disappeared. I began to see myself not as a free man, but a slave. I looked up Good Old Tom. I didn't have any money, but he knew where there was a party. I went.

The third time I took LSD, the people I was tripping with and I decided to take a whole pill. I mean, a pill is a pill. No more halves for us. So four of us took 1 pink tab each. We got off listening to our music, but we didn't get off like being really high on grass, or like the shimmering trips I had taken before. We went off like spaceships blasting into the stratosphere.

Within an hour of taking the drug, I could no longer see the people I was in the room with. My eyes looked into a sea of squirming orange stars, which moved about like the amoeba I had once seen in a microscope. There was no reaching or talking through the stuff. I was drowning in it, and I was drowning alone. No one could help me, and no one even knew I was drowning. I was completely freaked out. I was yelling, screaming at the top of my lungs, "I've got to come down! I've got to get down!"

Unfortunately, my friends couldn't help. I think Chuck was looking for a way to kill himself. His girlfriend was curled in a fetal ball in the corner, sobbing. Jim, our host and provider of the pink tabs, was intently pursuing an intimate conversation with his sister who had died three years before.

As I looked up, I saw the face of the Devil laughing at me and saw my life turned into an isolated world, where no human contact was possible. It was a world which I would be forced to live in for an eternity.

I sensed that if I did not will myself to breathe, I would stop. Intently, I listened for the continuous thumping of my heart, knowing that as long as I heard it, I was alive.

I drifted away, and two hours later found myself in the bed, tripping at a very enjoyable level. We had a great time, but I still felt the breath of the Devil.

I knew I had seen the edge. I had gone over and somehow come back, but the mystery of why I had come back eluded me. I took three tranquilizers I got from a friend and slept again. But I woke up shaken, and to a certain extent have been shaken ever since. I am certain that since then, I have been a markedly different person. LSD blew my brain that day, shredded it like a cheap tire.

I stayed with my new friends. They were rich kids and didn't need to work, and they liked my company. I lost contact with Dennis, but I did hear from Good Old Tom that he was "slave dancing with Mr. Brownstone," tying your arm and sticking it in - sharing your dope and your blood.

But I had a few breaths left. Can you believe I wanted to try it "one more time?"

For weeks I couldn't tell the difference between reality and imagination. When a street light changed color, I would have to ask myself, "Is that for real, or am I just hallucinating again?"

Time didn't matter anymore. When we had the stuff, we used it - day or night. A friend came to the pad with a couple of pieces of paper about an inch square. They looked so innocent, but they had on them our special rocket to another world. We sat down, and with the fear of another bad trip, but hope for euphoria and escape, I placed the piece of paper soaked in LSD on my tongue. I chewed it for awhile and even before I could spit it out, a jolt hit me. Lights began to blind me, red became a brighter red. I put on my earphones, and the music began to transport me out of this ugly old world into beautiful rooms where the walls started talking.

I don't know how long it lasted, but we decided we needed some fresh air. I don't know how we got to the park. I guess we walked. While leaning back on a bench I heard one of my friends scream, "He's dying, he's dying." Who's dying," I yelled, and realized they couldn't hear me. I realized I was actually lying on my back, choking, or thought I was, and screaming for help. But no one could hear me. I looked up and there I stood, kind of fuzzy, but there I was look-

ing down at myself choking to death. I tried
to get up but my body, the one on the
ground, wouldn't move. My friends were
yelling, "He's gone, Oh my God, he's gone!" I
can't put into words the terrible fear. All I
could think was that I had died and gone to
hell - and this was what hell was like. You
scream and no one can hear you. You try to
move and can't and all the while you are
standing there - at least one of you - looking
down at the other you. The darkness and
fear grew worse, but suddenly I looked up
and there was the tattooed dude, crouched
over me, face close to mine, feeling my neck.
No one else seemed to see him. He stuck his
fingers into my mouth and cleaned the
vomit out of my throat. Then he placed his
mouth on mine and began to breathe into
me. Slowly, the part of me that was standing began to return to my body. I screamed.
I choked and began to breathe fresh air. I
was alive.

   After lying on the ground for a long
time, I slowly got up. I wanted to thank the
man, but couldn't find him. My friends left
finally, wandering off, and I sat alone for a
long time. Finally, I made a decision. I did-
n't have a penny. There was an old couple
sitting on a bench. They looked nervous as I
half stumbled towards them, and they started to get up as I said, "It's OK. I was just
wondering if I could borrow money for a

telephone call." They looked relieved, and the woman dug in her purse, handed me a quarter and asked, rather anxiously, "Are you sure that's enough."

I didn't have to ask Grams if I could come home. After repeating my name, it was the first thing she said, and that she would come and pick me up in front of the Greyhound bus depot.

About a half-hour later I heard a horn beep and my name called. Pastor Barnes called out the window, "Hey Randy, you need a ride home? Get in."

So here I am, with my thesaurus, my life, and my pillow behind my head, realizing I went looking for a deliverer and found a deceiver. And so my search goes on.

Your son, I guess,

August 12, 1996

Dear Dad,

Well it feels good to finally be sleeping at a place where I don't have to always be watching my back. The only time I have to watch it now is when Grams rubs it.

I've been so tired lately, and I'm not sure why. Maybe my body is longing for a quick escape, but I'm not quite sure. Grams keeps trying to get me to go out and do things with her, but I just want to sleep.

Yesterday I went to bed at 7:30 at night and I didn't wake up until 2:00 the next afternoon. I think Grams thinks I might still be on something, but I swear I'm clean.

I wish we could talk man to man right now. I could really use some advice and direction, not the kind that Grams gives, but decisions about my future that only you can really help me with. Like if I should go back to school? Should I join the Navy like you did? What do I want to do with my life?

I'm really confused, Dad. I want to do the right thing and make the right decisions, but I'm not sure how.

I'm tired.

Your sleepy son,

Randy

November 1, 1996

Dear Dad,

Today is my birthday. You'd think that after all these years I'd stop looking, but I did it again this year.

The excitement that something might actually be there isn't as strong as it was a couple of years ago, but still for a split second as I open up the mailbox, my heart pounds thinking this might be the year that I hear from you.

I'm not hoping for an expensive present, just a card; to see your writing, with your broken R; maybe catch a scent of your Old Spice, to know that you were thinking of me, if even only for the few seconds it took to sign my card.

My friend's dad left him too, but a couple of times a year he sends him cards, and signs them, "Love, Dad." He keeps all those cards between his mattress, I think he sleeps better having those cards under there, having it in writing that his dad loves him.

Well, I've got to go, Grams has a cake and some candles for me. I'm still feeling pretty sick though. I must be really sick if I don't feel like eating Gram's cake.

B' boy,

Randy

March 11, 1997

Dear Dad,

Right now I'm staring at the ceiling, writing by the light of the streetlight. I'm not sure how to digest what I heard today. I've been feeling really tired and sick lately, and Grams finally made me go to the doctor last week where they did a bunch of tests. They called today with the results.

Dad, I'm not sure how it happened. I know I've done a lot of stupid things these past couple of years, but I didn't do anything to deserve this. The doctor told me that they have new treatments, and drug "cocktails" and the future is looking much brighter for people like me. I've never felt as alone as I do right now. Grams doesn't know. How do you tell an old woman that the only person she has left in the world to share life with has AIDS?

Randy

August 20, 1997

Dear Dad,

Here I sit at one-thirty in the morning with my head, as usual, propped up against a pillow. But some things have changed. I got a haircut at Grams' gracious encouragement. She says it's good to see my eyes sparkle again.

I saw Mrs. Myers, not at school, but Grams invited her to the house. She told me she heard that I wasn't doing well, but that she kept praying that nothing would happen to me big enough to take that infectious smile off my face. She said that even though I'm sick she is sure her prayers were answered.

But when I was alone, the loneliness and anger were still there. When I looked at Ken Griffey, Jr., still partly missing, the anger would swell up, but there was something different. I spent a lot of time, not feeling sorry for myself, but analyzing where I had been, what I had done. I had to. I had to keep busy. I knew my "friends" - those wrapped up in a cigarette paper, a syringe or dropped on a square of paper - were ready and waiting.

Some of the things I learned began to help. I realized that when you feel you're right and the world is wrong, there are more things to hate than the day has hours. When you only hate, and you can only handle so much, you separate your life into what you can see, and shoot, snort or swallow them up one at a time.

When you are afraid of the past, but frozen in fear of the future, you live by the hour and create life on the spot: "All that matters is me and this minute, and to hell with everybody and everything else."

I realized I couldn't think rationally anymore. I couldn't hold my thoughts for more than a few minutes, and even in those thoughts everything was all screwed up. I couldn't tell beauty from ugliness, happiness from sadness.

The last thing I wanted was for someone to guide me, but little by little I realized that when there is no authority, we become more and more the captives of each other. Peer control takes over. I thought I was my own boss. I left home, but I found out I didn't control my life at all. My peers and our mutual anger did. My drugs controlled me, and instead of being fulfilled, my soul became terminally ill and more lonely than I ever thought possible.

In the most basic terms, I threw away 16 months of my life. You have to be a first-class fool to make that kind of a deal. I was everything I accused you of being.

But what was I to do? I kept alone as much as possible. In the evening I would sit out on the porch, and when I felt well enough would go for walks. Grams would look worried when I went out, and always managed to be up, working in the kitchen, when I returned.

I walked where I knew I wouldn't run into any old friends. While passing an old industrial park late one night, I saw a bunch of kids about my age come out of a building, talking, laughing, having fun. Been a long time since I'd laughed or had fun. I went the other way.

A week later I went by the same place. They kind of looked like the party type. I got close enough to see a sign: "Committed Fellowship." I wondered if this is where crazy kids hung out.

I saw a donut shop down the street, so I walked down and got a Coke - the kind you drink. I was really there to ask about the place where the kids hung out.

I tried to be casual when I commented to the clerk that it must be a nuisance to have all those wild kids down the street.

He looked surprised. "Oh no, they're no trouble. They're great. They come up here and get donuts, and when I open on Sunday they even put up signs, 'Parking for

Donuts Only,' in front of my place. Good bunch of kids." He looked at me and half-smiled, "Wish they had been around when my boys were growing up."

I took my Coke and donut and walked down to the place, and a truly amazing thing happened next. There was a guy inside leading the singing, and after he finished a song he started talking to the people and thanking them for their prayers and their love for him. I recognized his physical features, for they were just like mine when I looked in the mirror. His skinny frame and his accompanying cane told me that maybe I wasn't the only one here who was sick.

He went on and told the people that even though he wasn't sure what was going on with his body and sometimes this world made him feel like an outcast, he had a peace that was greater than all of his fears and questions. He cleared his throat and sang a simple song. I didn't quite know what it meant, but I knew I needed it.

"In the morning when I rise," he softly sang, "Give me Jesus."

"And when I am alone,"
"Give me Jesus."

"And when I come to die,"

"Give me Jesus."

And then as if he saw and felt some wonderful secret that only he and someone else knew, he sang out like he meant it.

"Give me Jesus, Give me Jesus."

Over and over he sang these words, crying, but not sad tears.

I had to get out of there because I thought I was going to lose it and start crying myself. Outside I saw a kid about my age keeping an eye on the parking lot. When he looked up and saw me, he walked over and asked me if I needed any help. I told him no, then sort of blurted out, "How do I get Jesus?" He smiled gently, and we sat down at the end of the planter. He looked at me, and said, "You want Jesus?"

I don't know why, but before he could say any more, I asked if they had a cure for loneliness. He set his flashlight down and said, "Man, let me tell you a story. I gotta feeling you will know what I'm talking about, because I know exactly where you've been. Ever read the Bible?"

"Yeah," I said, "but it's been a long time."

"Well, in the Bible..." Then he told me about a man who had been sick for a long time. Not only was he sick, but he liked to hang around with people who were just as sick as he was.

One day a Stranger walked up to the sick man and fixed his penetrating, love-filled eyes on him. He asked him, "Mister, do you really want to get well?"

"Yeah, sure, said the man. Can't you see that's why I'm here?"

The Stranger repeated the question with emphasis on the word "really." "But do you REALLY want to get well?"

The man said, "That's a stupid question. Of course I do. Do you think I enjoy living with all these sick people? All I ever hear are complaints of how ugly life is and how we can't help it, and how bad our luck is. You think I like this kind of life? No way, man!"

The Stranger talked almost as if he didn't hear what the man had said. Sternly, in slow, distinct words, the Stranger said, "Let me ask you again. Do you really want to get well or do you kind of enjoy your affliction? Are you kind of getting used to this lifestyle? Do you like to shock people with your differences? Do you like to make people who have food feel guilty because you don't have any? Do you like not having any responsibilities?"

Suddenly, the man felt a surge of hope like he had never felt before. "No," he said,

"I really do want to get well. Everything you said about me is true. But deep down inside, I want to get well. I want to be healed." And then he fell at the Stranger's feet and begged, "Please help me."

Then, before I knew what I was doing, I said, "You're right. That *is* my story." The next thing I knew, I was sobbing, my face in my hands, and this man, this kid, this stranger, had his hands on my shoulders and was praying. "Jesus, don't be a stranger to this brother any longer. He wants to be healed. Heal him now. Come into his life. Fill whatever vacuum there is. Help this crippled young man to pick up his bed and walk out of here, never to look back again with envy."

As he was praying - I swear this is the truth - I felt heat go from his hands throughout my body. For a second I thought, *Oh no, I'm tripping again.* But this was different. It was like a warm shower, cleaning away all the filth. I don't know how long it took, but when I stood up, I felt clean all over. After we had talked a while longer, and I was turning to leave, the guy said, "I sure hope I see you again."

That night Dad, I was healed. Not from the AIDS and the pain that goes with it, but from a pain that I thought would be with me for eternity.

I walked out of that parking lot and

started home. Maybe I ran. My legs don't work that well anymore, but for a moment I didn't feel the pain. When I opened the front door, Grams was in the kitchen. She looked at me with fear all over her face, and then I did something I had never done before. I went over, took Grams in my arms, and began to cry. We cried together. I told her all about it. We cried some more, then I went into my room and like the old days, when we got home late from the ball game, I barely hit the bed before I went to sleep. The last sound I heard was Grams on the phone, crying tears of joy.

Love from your new born son,

Randy

November 7, 1997

Dear Dad,

Well, here I am, propped up against the wall, a pillow behind my head, all my medication taken, and my yellow pad on my lap.

Grams and I just finished watching Jay Leno. We do it a couple nights a week. We laughed together at his monologue. What Grams doesn't get, I explain to her. She just brought me a big glass of milk and some homemade oatmeal cookies.

I've come to some important conclusions.

First, my primary problem wasn't the broken home that you created. My primary problem was that I allowed myself to become a victim. I can see that very clearly now. I'm not going to pull any punches though, Dad. I'm willing to accept my share of the responsibility for what happened in my life, if you're willing to accept yours. I made some very poor choices; choices that caused me and those around me a great deal of harm. But it was you who forced me into those choices. You pulled the world out from under Mom and me when you left, and put us into situations that we would have never seen had you kept your word and stayed with us.

I'd like to see you and talk to you about all of this, now that so many years have gone by. Sometimes I still get mad at you for leaving me without any warning, just washing your hands of me. I'd like to ask you why you left, if you are happier now, what you are doing. I promise that I won't bug you. Maybe we could just meet for a half hour and have a Coke together, like the old days, and then I'll be on my way. After all of this, it still would mean a lot to me to know that you are still proud to call me Son.

Grams gave me the number where you work, so maybe I can call you and set up a time.

Grams says she'll let me borrow some money so that when I feel a little better I can fly down and see you. I'm looking pretty skinny, but I still look a lot like you did in your old black and white Navy picture.

One final word from my one final letter. I'd like to be able to really explain what has happened to me these last couple of weeks, but the words aren't there, except to say, the loneliness is gone and so is the anger.

I hope you won't be jealous if I tell you I've found a new Father, not a dad, but a Father who is a true Father to the fatherless generation.

At Committed Fellowship the other night, the guy who leads the singing sang a song that I can't stop thinking about -

The day I left home
I knew I'd broken his heart
I wondered then if things
would ever be the same

Then one night
I remembered his love for me
And down on that dusty road
Ahead I could see

And the only time
The only time
The only time I ever saw Him run

And then He ran to me
Took me in his arms
Held my head to His chest
And said my son's come home again

Looked at my face
Wiped the tears from my eyes
With forgiveness in His voice
He said, Son do you know I still love you?

It caught me by surprise
It brought me to my knees

When God ran

I saw Him run to me
And then I ran to Him

I can't wait until this song comes true. How
I long for a Father to run to.

Hopefully I'll see you soon,

Randy

The effect was eerie and surrealistic as the red revolving light on top of the ambulance cast a pulsating glow across an otherwise peaceful, rain covered landscape.

A van, its windows blackened, pulled up behind the ambulance and skidded a few inches in the rain. The front door opened and an officious young man, dressed in a parka and boots, walked into the house.

He joined the paramedics and a policeman as they looked down at the young man.

His head, covered by a black navy stocking cap, was leaning comfortably against a pillow. He had on a blue navy pea coat which looked freshly pressed. His eyes were closed, and on his face was a look of perfect peace, a half smile frozen on his lips. He looked like millions of young men sleeping on any given morning, waiting for their mothers to call them for breakfast. "Whatta we got here?" asked the coroner.

"His grandma said he had AIDS."

"Looks like he was planning on going somewhere."

"I found these on him," he said, handing the coroner a thesaurus and two bundles of letters tied together.

The officer pointed to the top envelope. "The R's on the address, plus the R on the REFUSED and the RETURN TO SENDER are all written the same way, with broken strokes. None have been opened. Strange."

"Is that all?" asked the coroner, thumbing through the unopened envelopes.

"No. I took these out of his hands, a pen and a yellow pad with this letter."

They read it together.

November 16, 1997

Dear Father,

This is my last letter. I think I'll be seeing you very soon. I have to tell you, I feel wonderful...so peaceful. The rain is falling. I feel clean, just like the rain, inside and out. The anger is gone, the fear, and most of all the loneliness. I can almost feel Your hand on my shoulder.

A very special warmth has overtaken me...I can't explain it in words, but I can feel it...there are some tears. They are warm on my face.

Don't worry about the fatted calf. I've eaten more than my share of my inheritance. I want You to hug me and tell me You love me. That will do, and then I can be Your servant.

I'm coming home...

Your ever loving son,

Randy

P.S. Could you do me one favor? Remind Mom I'll be home for Thanksgiving dinner. Thanks.

EPILOGUE

God established the family as His first institution and as the building block of society with the creation of Adam and Eve, which was recorded by Moses in Genesis 2:24-25. In Deuteronomy chapters 6-11, God established the timeless principle that a nation's (and a family's) success is directly related to its obedience to God. In Deuteronomy 6:5-9, Moses wrote:

You shall love the Lord your God with all your heart, with all your soul, and with all your might.

And these words which I commanded you today shall be in your heart;

You shall teach them diligently to your children, and you shall talk of them when you sit in your house, when you walk by the way, when you lie down, and when you rise up.

You shall bind them as a sign on your hand, and they shall be as frontlets between your eyes.

You shall write them on the doorposts of your house and on your gates.

Without a personal relationship with the true and living God of the Bible, parents really have nothing to give their children to properly equip them for the future. Without a personal relationship with Jesus Christ, parents can only give their children things that will last, in the ideal situation, for a physical lifetime.

With a personal relationship with the Messiah, however, parents can equip their children for an eternity.

The modern American family is under the most fierce spiritual and social attack in our nation's history. Our economic, educational, and media systems have stacked the odds so high against the family that only a remnant of the traditional, God-fearing family remains.

If parents, especially fathers, neglect their responsibility to raise their children to know Jesus personally and to equip them in the ways of the Lord, they will fail in the greatest task set before them, no matter how successful they appear in the eyes of the world.

A prayerful study of the lives of Eli the priest in 1 Samuel 1-4, Solomon the king in 1 Kings 1-11 and the Book of Ecclesiastes, and the final decline of the nation of Israel in the Book of Malachi clearly demonstrate that corruption first begins on a personal level, and then quickly spreads to the levels of family, religion, government, and nation. The ultimate result is a curse by God, instead of a blessing. God's disfavor is removed only by repentance and through a personal relationship with the Son of God, that is, Jesus Christ.

The bottom line in our nation's sad state of affairs is the lack of personal knowledge of and commitment to God and the things of God, as given to us in the Bible, his unchanging Word. Until men humble themselves and seek the face of God, searching His Word in truth and honesty, they will never know how to be fathers, husbands and men in the way God intends for them to be.

May all of us cry out to God with the simple voice of Carl Lawrence's Randy, "I want you to hug me and tell me you love me," so that we, in turn, might answer the same cries of our children.

Raul Ries

Credits

When God Ran, Benny Hester / Word Publishing

Give me Jesus, Public Domain

Photos: Jeremy Dodgen/Dodgen Photography